TOWARDS SUCCESS

Roohi Soni

Invincible Publishers

First published in India in 2018

ISBN: 978-93-87328-99-0

Invincible Publishers

G-120, Sushant Lok III, Sector 57, Gurgaon-122002

Registered Address: Opposite Kasturba Ashram, Radaur, Haryana - 135133

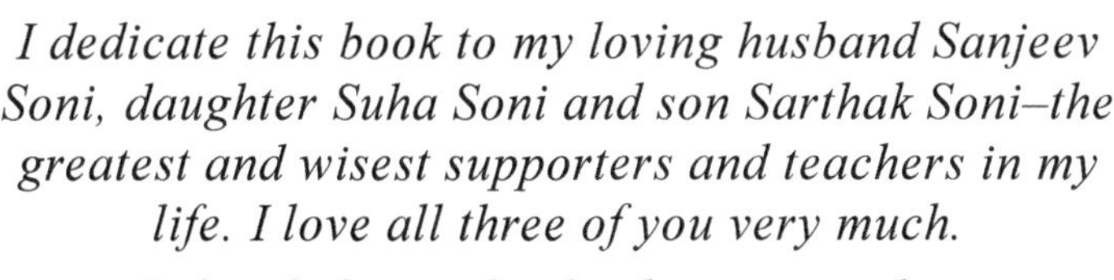

I dedicate this book to my loving husband Sanjeev Soni, daughter Suha Soni and son Sarthak Soni–the greatest and wisest supporters and teachers in my life. I love all three of you very much.

I also dedicate this book to my readers.

Acknowledgement

First of all, I am thankful to the Almighty, the invisible force, that drove me to jot down this book. Whenever I felt blank during the course of writing this book, His divine presence encouraged me to write on. I am thankful to my husband whose constant support made me write and finish the book. Despite a hectic schedule at the court every day, his curious eyes inquire about the progress of my book daily. He has always wanted me to achieve something different.

I am thankful to my daughter who was always ready to help me in one way or the other during my journey to complete this book. She had full confidence that her mom will write and finish the book well in time. Talking to me daily from her hostel, she inquired regularly about the progress of the book.

I am highly thankful to my son. When I first started writing the book, I had very less experience of typing. Initially, I dictated a few pages to him, which he typed out very patiently. Whenever he came back from the university, his first question to me was always, "What have you written today, mom?"

Thanks once more to all the members of my family for believing, encouraging and supporting me. I am thankful to my father, whose life is itself an example. He is an independent man even today at the age of 76.He is full of energy and enthusiasm and works like a man of thirty five.

I am thankful to my [late] mom, who always wanted to make me a perfect woman in all fields of life ever since my childhood.

I am thankful to my brother and sister-in-law for believing in me.I am also thankful to my little niece for having great trust in me. I give special thanks to my mother-in-law, who taught me the basic things that are necessary for a girl to adjust in life along with her profession. I am thankful to my late father-in-law, who was always curious to see me at the top of my profession. He believed in my abilities and was a great source of inspiration for me.

I am thankful to all my relatives who always encouraged and appreciated me being different from the clan. I am thankful to all our family friends. I am also thankful to the friends of my children, who are always curious to know what I am doing next.

I am very thankful to Mr.Ajay Setia, who accepted my manuscript on my very first phone call. I am thankful to Ms. Aditi Saxena, the editor, who really worked hard on my script. I am thankful to the entire team of Invincible Publishers for being very supportive and encouraging throughout the process of publishing.

Lastly, I thank you, dear reader, for picking up this book. If even a single line from this book touches your heart, my purpose of writing it would stand fulfilled.

My ‘thank you’ list is very long, but I sum it up here.

Foreword

The idea of writing a book rarely comes as it is difficult project, but actually writing a book is extremely difficult. Mrs. Roohi Soni has done it inspite of her busy schedule as an advocate. She really deserves congratulations.

I know Mrs. Soni as a daughter of one of my colleagues. She has worked as the President of District Consumer Disputes Redressal Forum, Bhatinda with distinction. All good works can be expected from her.

Mrs. Soni has penned down the book with 21 chapters besides a Prologue and an Epilogue. These chapters contain different moods of life and some of these chapters are titled as 'Inner beauty of self', 'The Value of thoughts', 'Look deeper inside yourself', 'Your planning and His planning' and other chapters have been given different titles. Her idea is to tell the readers how to make one's life happy in this beautiful world. It is a philosophical book and each chapter contains a beautiful idea followed by examples which shows that thoughtful ideas are not merely vague and fiction but everyone who follows these principles can make one's life happy. For example, she has written Chapter 13 as "Pain is inevitable, but suffering is optional". The universal truth is that pain is an unavoidable part of life but how one takes it, whether he cries or he assigns the pain to the God and feels satisfied, makes all the difference in the way of life.

Even Swami Vivekanand has said, "All power is within you, you can do anything and everything, believe in that, do not believe that you are weak". He further said, "Stand up, be bold and be strong. Take the whole responsibility on your own shoulders, and know that you are the creator of your own destiny."

Human Life is the rare gift given by the God to us, the human beings. The human beings are entirely different from other beings created by the God on the earth like animals, in the air like birds and the insects and in the sea like fishes, etc. If inspite of having the privilege of getting the human life, one does not become constructive and fails to leave anything memorable when he leaves the world, it would be like a proverb, "A man has lived as if he was never born and he has died as if he has never lived".

Mrs. Soni has really done a wonderful work and any reader cannot ignore to follow the principles enunciated by her in this book if they want to make their life worth living.

Mrs. Soni deserves congratulations for such a fabulous work with glorious and relevant examples.

I hope that this book would succeed and would reach the hands of maximum readers.

I wish Mrs Soni and the book all the success.

Justice S.N.Aggarwal

When you were born,
Your parents welcomed you.
Now it's time for you
To welcome yourself.
To celebrate your birth on this planet,
Treat your soul with the best qualities.

Index

Prologue

Create whatever you want in your life. Read the holy books as many times as you want, but not under any compulsion. Try to understand each and every line of the holy books. Each and every word conveys a message to you. Don't make others follow what you say, follow what you say yourself first. Act upon the message given in the holy books. The preachers covey these teachings to others, but they themselves have adopted the same into their lives too; if not, there is no need of preaching, recitation.

Your destiny is in your hands. You can add or subtract whatever you want from it. Positive thoughts take you towards positive persons, while negative thoughts take you towards negativity. Thoughts travel, reach and stick to the person for whom you have created them. Don't create bad thoughts for yourself. Be clear and honest to yourself, so that all the others will be clear and honest to you too. You never know who is more saintly–a person sitting inside the temple, or one standing outside. Respect yourself.

Life is a river–let it flow despite the various hindrances that come in its way. You will reach your destination. The values of your nature make it easier to cross all the hurdles of your life. Raise the standard of your thinking. Love the people around you. Respect your feelings, and the feelings of others. My life has a meaning, so does yours. My time is precious, so is yours. My life is bliss, so is yours. My children are precious for me, so are yours.

Life is a journey; complete it with grace and respect. It does not matter how long you've lived, but how you've lived. It does not matter where you live, but how many hearts you have made your place in. It does not matter how many times you've cried, but how many people had tears rolling down their eyes after you.

Life is bliss, live it. Care for, love and respect your spouse, your life partner, who holds your hand through all the ups and downs in your life. Love your parents who have no children besides you. Love your children, who have no parents besides you. Hold your relations with importance don't let them fall out easily. Be patient with the new relations who may not be able to understand you. It's not important how many people appreciated you, but how many people are appreciated by you. You are enough to appreciate yourself. Start appreciating yourself, and the world will appreciate you.

Chapter 1

INNER BEAUTY OF THE SELF

Your inner self is very beautiful, which means that you have a great positive thinking full of all the basic qualities that a child has since birth to the age of about five or six years. Every soul is beautiful, if you see through the eyes of your beautiful mind. Your inner self is the most beautiful thing as you can control, channelize, turn and change it. You can make your world beautiful by making simple changes to it. When you want to check the beauty of your inner self, try to calm your mind from all the bad thoughts, vices, ill-wills, etc.

When your mind is stressed, it automatically becomes confused. Think about the moments when you were happy to see things going in your favour. Inner self is nothing but the sub-conscious mind where good thoughts and feelings come automatically. Your soul is pure. Check it by simple methods. You are a peaceful, happy, contended, loveable, pure, powerful and knowledgeable soul; these are the basic qualities which you already possess. But with the fast moving world, your daily tasks have taken you away from all these qualities. Just relax your mind and body.

Sit in a place where you feel the most comfortable. Try to feel that you are only with yourself and nobody else. Then, think about those people who have ever made you feel happy and good. Also think about those moments of your life which made you feel satisfied and contended. Forget or set aside those thoughts that corrupt your mind throughout the day. Avoid those persons whose presence disturbs you. You are not here to think badly of anyone. You are a very pious soul, full of love, compassion, satisfaction etc. Withdraw yourself from bad ideas and feelings.

You are a royal soul. As you know, in the olden days, kings and queens, emperors and empresses wore such expensive, glittering, clean and attractive attires with expensive jewels embroidered into their robes, as well as beautiful and attractive ornaments all over their body. Such should be your soul. It should wear jewels made out of the purest of stones, which are in fact metaphors for the basic qualities of a soul–purity, peace, love, knowledge and happiness. Your soul has the power to discriminate, adjust, cooperate, face, tolerate, withdraw and judge. When you shall decorate your soul with such jewels and inculcate these values in your life, the inner beauty of your soul will shine through. The serenity on your face shall be full of glow, grace and eternity, while your expressions remain calm and full of love.

Now the question arises, how should these be practiced in your daily life? For that, one has to work on one's mind. Ask yourself the question, "Did I hurt anybody today, knowingly or unknowingly?”,”Have I cheated on anybody?”,”Have I been wrongful to them?”, etc. You have to check your mind daily. Work on each value every day. Day by day, as you start giving time to yourself, your inner beauty will shine through like a star. Slowly, you will learn how to control your mind. Your subconscious mind has an abundance of power and the solutions to solve all kinds of problems of this world.

Just relax and let it decide the finest things for you in your life. It is only possible if your conscious mind gives a good feedback to your subconscious mind. What your conscious mind thinks, it stores all those things in your mind. The right and good thoughts give you fruitful results, and good feelings enhance the beauty of your mind and face. Inner beauty of the soul can automatically be seen on one’s face. You can do so with meditation as well. Meditation is first talking to yourself, then the creator. Meditation is the medicine for all your sufferings, whether physical or mental.

Start working from today itself to enhance the inner beauty of yourself. For meditation, sit quietly for 15-20 minutes each day. Your entire focus and attention should be on your breathing. Quietly follow each breath as it enters and leaves your body. If your mind is wandering, try to focus again on only one thing, then bring it back from your worries and useless over-thinking. This can be done anywhere, regardless of whether it’s your house, your office, a park or wherever you feel comfortable.

A thought provoking message by Lord Buddha– Meditation brings wisdom, lack of meditation leaves ignorance. Know well what leads you forward and what holds you back and choose the path that leads to wisdom.

Every sane person in this world is well aware of his/her positive and negative qualities. This realization will take form if you check your mind again and again. When you feel good about someone, your mind is full of joy. When you help someone, you really feel very happy and satisfied. Your mind appreciates you for doing good. That is the inner beauty of the self. When your mind is full of useless thoughts, you tend to fall prey to egoism, selfishness and other unnecessary conceptions. You can never think of doing good to another person then. You cannot think of helping others. In such situations, your mind becomes supportive of your misbehavior. You can then call your mind sick.

Your mind is well aware of what you are doing, but you do such things while going against the basic qualities of your soul. I am not talking about those who are in the habit of doing wrong to others and always think badly about others; they are on a wrong frequency altogether. Here, I am referring to those persons who want to change and enhance the beauty of their self. You must have noticed how people change their habits and improve themselves. In this book, the journey is towards such a change, a transformation of the soul.

A person passes through various stages during his/her of life. During this journey, he meets with many challenges and chooses the emotions for himself, the thoughts that he wants to live with creates an imaginary world for himself and is still unaware that he is creating his own destiny, his own world–good or bad. We all do that. If you live with good thoughts and try to put those in action, it is the beauty of your inner self. If you are sowing and growing bad thoughts and make them a part or style of your life, it will contaminate your mind and blind your soul, just as dust and fog make the window panes dirty and blur the visibility through them. Likewise, when the mind is polluted by unnecessary thoughts, it shows everything negative to you and takes you towards pessimism and depression.

On the other hand, if you are optimistic in life, it takes you towards happiness. Your mind is full of good qualities. Do not let dust and fog pollute them. Clean your thoughts from time to time. Groom your mind well. Plant and water the seeds of good thoughts. Your inner self will always guide you to do better things in life. It determines your behavior, mood and conduct with others. Check your inner beauty from time to time. No one else can help you with this. Change will come about only if you decide to change yourself. Mahatma Gandhi said, “Be the change that you wish to see in the world,” and once you do it, your life will change.

All human beings possess some special talent and are here for some special purpose .Each one of us is here for a noble cause that will allow us to achieve our highest potential. Try to do your best in adding value to the lives around you. Recognize your inner skills, talents and potential. You are sufficient to change yourself. Become a serene and tranquil person. Be grateful to the creator that you are ‘serene and tranquil’. This gives you inner peace and enhances your inner beauty, the reflection of which will always be seen on your face. Your physical condition will also improve with the inner beauty of the self.

"If a person's basic state of mind is serene and calm then it is possible for this inner peace to overwhelm a painful physical experience."–The Dalai Lama.

Exercise 1

Your mind is beautiful. To check the inner beauty of the self, write down your good qualities honestly.

For example: I don't lie, whatever the situation may be.

1.
2.
3.
4.
5.
6.
7.
8.

Being happy is your right and a good quality as well. Make the list of qualities which you feel make your mind peaceful and happy.

1.
2.
3.
4.
5.
6.
7.

Chapter 2

THE VALUE OF THOUGHTS

"Keep your thoughts positive because your thoughts become your words, keep your words positive because your words become your behavior, keep your behavior positive because your behavior becomes your habits, keep your habits positive because your habits become your values, keep your values positive because your values become your destiny," said Mohandas Karamchand Gandhi.

Thoughts are what you feel feelings are the shadows of your thoughts. You have good and bad thoughts daily, which turn into feelings. Sometimes, the bad thoughts are so dominant that they give you bad feelings and destroy the day, week, month, or even years of your life. You need to take a break and check the status of your mind. Will you let your whole precious life be spoilt in bad thoughts? Like an untamed horse, your mind keeps giving you thoughts which have no relevance in your life. These bad thoughts lead bad feelings in too.

Change the frequency of your thoughts. Like a tower that continuously gives signals to your mobile phone, your mind also gives you non-stop signals or frequencies. These are recorded in the universe, while the law of attraction gives the same thoughts back to you. Put a full-stop on your bad thoughts in this moment itself, today is the best moment to shun them out. You might never want any negativity in your life intentionally, but you continuously keep attracting it with your bad thoughts which exhaust your brain, make you feel tired, sick, sleepy, lonely, depressed, etc.

Come out of it right this moment. You can be out of it within half a second just by changing your thought process. Start thinking positively, ignore the things and the persons that you don't like, take a break try to believe in the notion 'Out of sight, out of mind'. Welcome the positive vibrations into your life with open arms. Embrace them, hug them tightly. Amend yourself. The whole world is yours and you will get whatever you want–peace, happiness, power, knowledge, courage, patience, tolerance, health, wealth, love, affection–in short, every positive thing in your life.

Develop a practice of checking your thoughts again and again. As a person with a sound mind continuously keeps his attention on the road while driving his car and tries to keep his own car as well as the other vehicles safe from any accident, you need to keep checking your thoughts similarly. What you experience all day through your thought process is mental traffic. You need to regulate and manage that mental traffic. Give a pause to your continuous thought process while, checking it time and again so that there is no derailment of any manner. Positive thoughts bring positivity, while negative thoughts bring negativity not only to your life, but also to the lives of others around you. Thoughts have a strong force that can change everything. Face the circumstances and people around you.

Thoughts are like rays emitting from a source of light. Darker the night, the brighter will be the day following it. The rays of light given off by the sun as well as their refractions have their limitations which have successfully been measured by scientists. They also study and measure the travelling time of sound and its frequency. Similarly, the measurement of thoughts is done by philosophers, but the ability to do so is not limited to them. Even a common man can measure the frequency and power of the mind's thoughts.

A lot of us have heard of telepathy. Telepathy is not a mythic system, but has a scientific logic behind it. You can experience it yourself through this experiment: Think of a person very strongly and passionately, and he/she will start responding to you, no matter where they are in the world at that time. Thoughts travel faster than light or sound. The latter have limitations, while our thoughts have no limitations, but can still be measured. If you think badly of anyone, the same thought is automatically created in the mind of that person about whom you are thinking badly. If you are praising someone and have a good opinion of him, that person will also be on the same frequency as you, and you will hear something good from him in return. Thoughts travel and come back to you. The traffic of thoughts is continuous throughout the day.

Your brain is so powerful that it can store the data of a hundred powerful computers in it. The memory of a computer and the number of files and folders contained in it is limited, but there are unlimited files and folders with an unlimited space to store your mind. The mind keeps working day and night. Thoughts, good and bad, are a continuous process of your life. The more the thoughts, the more you are disturbed. Learn to channelize them with some mind exercises. With focus and concentration, you will be able to control the free flow of the thoughts.

Your thoughts keep you occupied the whole day. Sometimes, you live in an imaginary world away from reality. Your thoughts make you cry and laugh. Learn to meditate; it will not only help you control your thoughts, but also reduce their number and create good and productive thoughts instead. Doing one task at one time with full concentration makes you perfect. Today's generation multitasks, but without any concentration or focus. Your mind cannot work on two projects together. Here, I don't mean that you can't work on two or more assignments together, but the result of such an endeavour will be average. For results par excellence, doing only one task at a time works best.

Meditation for only five to ten minutes daily can help you channelize your thoughts and your mind's unlimited energy in the right direction. In the name of 'Thought of the day', you must come across many quotes of well known and successful people from different fields. Yet, you must never have heard of a 'Thought of the week…fortnight, month, year or a century'. It's always a thought of the day. The thought of the day means inspiring words from a wise person, on which you have to deliberate throughout the day. You have to think upon it, analyze it. If your mind accepts it fully, apply it in your life. The thought of the day is the mantra which you can recite throughout the day, work upon it and follow it. If you cannot keep a particular thought in your mind for some time, get ready for the next good thought. Thoughts have a great value in your life they shape your life and destiny.

"Change your thoughts and you change your world," said Norman Vincent Paele.

When I was a young girl, I remember that during the morning prayer in my school, the headmistress had the practice of quoting a few popular thoughts and proverbs, which the students had to repeat after her in a loud voice. Of all the proverbs that we repeated after her, the one 'God helps those, who help themselves' has really worked for me as a life changing thought in my life. All the students present in the morning assembly at school used to recite these lines as loudly as they could. Similarly, the words 'God loves all' was meant to never allow us to do anything wrong in life, nor feel too alone, lonely or deserted. Such thoughts can change one's life.

Wille Nelson has beautifully said, "Once you replace your negative thoughts with positive ones, you will start having positive results."

When you are doing something with good intentions and pure thoughts, the supreme, the almighty, and the universe come hand in hand to create the best for you. 'He' creates a space for you, even if you and the whole world thinks that there is no space for you. You might have millions of competitors in your field, but you should just keep believing in your thoughts. You might have heard people say, "I have always done right to everybody, never thought anything bad about them, but all my efforts are futile still." Such type of thoughts, are a waste and need to be thrown out of your mind immediately. Make sure that your mind has no place for waste, sick, stale and dirty thoughts.

Good thoughts build up your personality. They start showing their effect on your face, gait and eyes, and become a part of your personality. When your thoughts are pure, each and every sentence from you can become an inspiring quote. The various quotes and inspiring words written on prominent places are nothing but thoughts of great minds. Enlarge your own mind so that it can create such good thoughts too. Sit with yourself for sometime without any internal or external disturbances. Let the flow of your thoughts come and go as usual, then put a pause on them and give your mind a creative assignment. Keep your mind busy with creative things so that your negative thoughts cannot control your mind anymore.

The people who won their minds went on to win the entire world too. Sow the seeds of those thoughts which can take you onwards on the journey of success and towards your ultimate goal. Soaring high in the sky is your right; soar high with good, positive and creative thoughts. Good thoughts create good vibrations which take you onwards on the path of achieving everything that you desire.

Successful persons understand the value of thoughts and constantly take care of their mind. They choose the best thoughts for themselves and become happier, wealthier and more successful in their life. Once you start monitoring your thoughts, you will observe the destructive or bad thoughts automatically withering away, leaving you on the path of pure thoughts.

Thoughts have the force to change your entire world. Be careful about your thoughts. Create thoughts in your mind corresponding to what you wish to become in your life. Doing well for others is not a duty it's a joy which increases your health and happiness.

Exercise 2

Put a full stop on your bad thoughts. Whenever you sit alone, check your thoughts and put a full stop on the bad and useless thoughts. Think something beautiful, creative and constructive in your life. Make a list of good thoughts that give you happiness. Believe in positivity and put good thoughts and ideas into practice.

List here:

1.

2.

3.

4.

5.

6.

7.

8.

…and so on…

Chapter 3

LOOK DEEPER INSIDE YOURSELF

Show your best qualities to yourself, your parents, spouse, children, friends and the world at large, especially to those who care for you the most. Hurting is very easy. While you hurt somebody, you may feel that you have won the conversation, but that is not all. You have instead lost one of the best qualities, i.e., grace. If you do not want to get carried away with time, let yourself be comfortable with what you have .One day, you will find that you have learnt to flow with time without any compromises. At the same time, you will find that time is flowing as per your desires.

When you wake up in the morning, try and search your heart for what it wants. Check whether it wants to hurt anybody- the answer should be 'No'. If your mind starts to search for somebody who has hurt you in the last few days or perhaps yesterday itself, command it immediately to stop having this feeling of hurt. Rather, forget that feeling of hurt forever and come out of it with a smile. You will feel light as a feather. Thereafter, start thinking about your good qualities with great honesty.

Don't worry we all have very good qualities – the need is to be honest with oneself. Don't focus too much on your bad qualities as you grow in your good qualities. The graph of your bad qualities will automatically go down. How honest you are with yourself decides your qualities. Sometimes, you are good with people other than your children, parents and relatives, and harsh with your own relations, which sometimes creates a gap difficult to fill. Here, you need to show your best qualities.

While you hurt someone with one word or a little force, you hurt yourself with double the force. Explore your good qualities instead, and find out the peace in your heart. List your good and bad qualities. Check yourself regularly on whether you are acting as per your good qualities. On the other hand, try to shun one bad quality daily. Make a comparison between your own good and bad qualities. As the list of good qualities grows, the list of bad qualities will become shorter and shorter with time, and you will find one day that all the bad qualities have faded away into non-existence.

One bad quality can spoil your whole life. Don't let it do so. Replace it with a good quality. Negative thinking gives birth to only bad qualities and irrational thinking. Try to change your thought process. Give your behavior a reason, whether good or bad.

A man used to be angry with his fellow workers and subordinates all the time and his behavior was even worse with his domestic help. He was very harsh. After scolding and abusing them, he used to wonder why his behavior was so rude, but then justify it with lame excuses to himself and the people around him, especially his family members. Whenever he was angry with his subordinates, he used to forget about their good qualities as well as his own good qualities. He was losing his personality day by day.

The man was not bad at heart at all. He was God-fearing, hard working and successful, but was never happy with his subordinates, his fellow workers or his domestic help. His subordinates who knew his nature well, wanted him to stay in office. They wanted to feel comfortable with him and love and respect him. The others with whom his behavior was harsh were tired of his behavior and wanted him to leave the workplace.

Ultimately, the man got transferred to another place and had to shift to another city along with his family. His subordinates, colleagues and others whom he was associated with and was good to, were unhappy with the news of his transfer, whereas the people in his office and his domestic help who were mentally tortured by him, were happy and thankful to God for this sudden change.

This situation was such that the man had to now shift in with his mother along with his entire family. He was retired from his previous assignment and had to cope with his family, his retired 70 years old mother and her domestic help. After moving in with his mother, his eyes opened to the truth which had resided inside him all this while. He asked himself, "Why was I so abusive with my subordinates for such a long time? Was I really a bad person?" and got the answers within himself.

The behavior of his father and step-mother in the past had left such a negative impact on his mind that he had been unable to cope with it. He was always mean to those who could not confront him or challenge his behavior in any way, but was very pleasant with the others at the same time. The members of his family were also disturbed by his wrong behavior. His children and wife often told him about the faults in his behavior, but he always became offensive at such a confrontation and told them, “You are taking the side of the outsiders without understanding their concern.”

When he started living at his mother’s house, he learned the truth that his behavior was condemned by his mother too, and that nobody would accept it anymore. So, he finally started looking for pure positive qualities inside himself. He started to work upon his positive qualities daily and stopped being negative. With slow practice, he changed his way of taking things and situations entirely, and started respecting the people who used to be the target of his bad behavior before. When he looked back at the journey of his bad behavior, he felt ashamed of himself and his attitude.

Today, the man is full of good qualities and his life is more relaxed and pleasing for himself as well as his family. All praise for his qualities!

For the transformation of one’s soul, one has to check the daily habits and change the negative qualities into positive ones. It is very easy to check your behavior. Wrong and negative thoughts create wrong and negative feelings. A right and positive thought creates positive feelings. When you help somebody, it is a positive gesture. It gives pleasure to your mind and soul, making you feel proud. On the other hand, when you hurt somebody, this gesture immediately affects and changes your mood, making you feel that you've lost something inside you.

Plant, water and nourish the seeds of good qualities, the bad will automatically vanish away. Bad qualities are stale, broken, torn, dry and without life–like the old, rotten and dry leaves of a tree during the season of autumn. They are shed so that new, beautiful, delicate, tender, pure and soft leaves can spring forth in their place. Your mind is akin to such a tree where new leaves of good and positive qualities need to keep springing forth.

How is one to filter one's good qualities?

You'll find the answer when you look at a child who is in between the ages of zero to three years. Observe his smile, feel the purity of his mind when he speaks, notice the blissfulness and contentment on his face, and the happiness on his forehead when he sees his parents around. He doesn't need very big things to be happy. The mere presence of his parents makes him happy. Love is everything for a child.

You too can feel pure from the inside, entirely blissful and happy with the presence of your creator near you. You are the most loveable person for your creator. Believe this and you'll gradually find everything to change and become positive, like the early morning rays of the sun that reach the Earth and touch your face to give you a soothing effect. Use the lessons that you have learned from your past to raise a new level of awareness and enlightenment. Make yourself strong enough to say 'no' to the negative things in life, which include negative thoughts, foods, places, behavior, etc. Invite the beautiful things in the form of thoughts into your mind. Talk to your heart deeply enough so that new seeds of positive vibes can be sown.

Exercise 3

Make the list of all your good and bad qualities. We all know about our good and bad qualities. Be honest to yourself.

Good qualities:

For example: I go for a walk daily.

1.
2.
3.
4.
5.
6.
7.
8.

Bad qualities:

For example: I never go for a walk.

1.
2.
3.
4.
5.
6.
7.
8.

Compare these qualities. The number of your good qualities may be a lot. Use more paper and list them. Work on your bad qualities and try to replace one bad quality at a time with a good quality. Set a period of one week to leave one bad quality and add a good quality. (Say, you are in the habit of biting your lips, then don't bite your lips for a week, instead do something good.)

Say you have the good quality of rising up early in the morning. Don't ever change it. If you never go out for walks, it is a bad quality. Even if it does not harm anybody, it harms you and your physical and mental health. You need to replace it with the good habit of going for a walk daily. Go ahead and make your own list.

Chapter 4

HOW TO EXPRESS GRATITUDE

'Gratitude is absolutely the way to bring more into your life.'

- Marci Shimoff

Start your day by saying, 'Thank You.' As soon as you first open your eyes in the morning, say 'thank you' to all the people and objects around you. First of all, say thanks to the universe, the invisible, the power behind you, the supreme soul, God. Again, say 'thank you' when your feet first touch the floor in the morning, say 'thank you' when you look at your spouse, siblings, kids, parents and all the people that you meet. Not only this, say 'thank you' to all the things you touch, feel, eat, smell, read, the nature, and all the things that you already have.

As you start this practice in your daily life, you will feel a major change in yourself. The number of things to be thankful about will increase. The words 'thank you' will improve your relationships. Your mind, thoughts, and feelings should be full of gratitude. This is a life changing mantra. As you add these words to your life, it will surely change your life. All the things which you desire will be attracted towards you with an increased force. By saying ‘thank you’, you feel thankful towards the universe, the invisible, the holy being, God.

Have gratitude for the environment and the atmosphere. If these two things are favourable you will encounter more such circumstances where these two aspects will be more and more comfortable for you. Even if these two things are not favourable, say ‘thank you’ as you learn a lot of lessons from them which make you wiser. Slowly and eventually, these two will become more favourable and comfortable.

Don’t complaint about anything. While complaining, you send out negative vibrations into the universe. The universe never created negative things for you; you create the negativity in your life yourself. Send out positive vibrations in the universe by choosing very good thoughts for yourself. First of all, say ‘thank you’ for everything that you already have in your life, and also to those things which are not in your possession yet. Always say ‘thank you’ to the things which you desire to get in your life and feel as if you already have them. By doing so, you will start receiving them. The time limit is not settled, as it all depends upon you– how keenly you desire something and how strong is your ‘thank you’ mantra.

There was once an old woman named Stella who was a slave .After her liberation, she was hired by a family to work at their house, where she remained for many years. Sitting in the kitchen, Stella would often fold her hands and gaze upwards, saying the prayer, “Thank you, lord, for my vittles.”

Dr. James Richmond was very young at that time. Unable to understand the meaning of 'vittles', he used to ask himself, 'Why does Stella do so?' One day, he asked Stella what vittles were.

"Food and drink," replied Stella.

Dr. James Richmond then said politely "We always give you food & drink, whether or not you are thankful for it"

Stella said, "Yes, we will always get our vittles, but it makes them taste better when we're thankful."

After that, she started narrating a story to Dr. Richmond that when she was a young girl, an old teacher taught her to always look for things to be grateful for. As soon as she woke up the next morning, she asked herself, "What is the first thing that I can be thankful for today?" Sometimes, the smell of coffee coming from the kitchen early in the morning found its way to her room. On those mornings, the aroma forced her to say, "Much obliged, Lord, for the coffee and much more obliged for the smell of it!"

Young Richmond grew-up and left home. One day, he received a message that Stella was dying. He returned home and found her in bed with her hands folded in the same manner as he had seen her at the kitchen table at his house many a times before. Dr. Richmond wondered what she could be giving thanks for at a time like this. As if reading his mind, she opened her eyes and looked at the faces around her bed. Shutting her eyes again then, she said quietly, "Much thankful, Lord, for such fine friends."

Dr. Richmond was deeply influenced by Stella's mystic ability to always find something to be thankful for. He had learnt a vital secret from this wise old woman that many people never learn throughout their lifetime. He learnt to be thankful in every situation and to be happy throughout his life.

Wallace Walter said, "The daily practice of gratitude is one of the conducts by which your wealth comes to you." For leading a happier, wealthier and blissful life, one must learn the art of gratitude. Make a list of things that you are thankful for. Once you start making the list, you will notice one day that it is indeed unending. Thank every moment of your life. You are here for a purpose. Thank the Almighty, for he has given you such a beautiful heart which can feel the pain of others and is ready to help them in all kinds of situations. Thank Him for all your organs.

Add it to your daily practice to start your day by making a list of thanks. Be grateful for whatever you have today. As you begin to think about all the things that you are grateful for in your life, you will feel more thoughts coming back for more things that you might be grateful for. Make a habit of saying 'thank you' to everyone and everything, no matter how small it is. Your gestures will attract all the good things which you have ever wished for in your life.

John F. Kennedy said, "As we express our gratitude, we never forget that the highest appreciation is not to utter words, but to live by them." When you make gratitude a habit and a part of your behavior, the best things will start coming into your life. When you feel obliged to everyone, even though they have not helped you ever, you will feel a great change in yourself as well as in their behavior. Your life will then have more peace and happiness. Don't get confused, just say thanks to everyone and be thankful for everything.

I am greatly impressed by this little poem written by the American author Richelle E. Goodrich in her book 'Slaying Dragons':

"Thank you for the day and night, for rainy spells and summers light,

Thank you for the skies of blue and puffy clouds in greyish hue.

Thank you for the giggle fests and midnight's cloak to hasten rest.

Thank you for tomorrow new and yesterday's tomorrow too.

Thank you for "I am glad we met" and also for "We haven't met yet".

Thank you for the peace of mind and a grateful soul doth always find".

Exercise 4

Make a long list of the persons who have ever helped you in any manner in your life. Start your list with the 'Almighty' who has sent you to this earth. Then, make a list of the things for which you are thankful. Like, "I am thankful for being here on this earth."

For example: Thank you, 'God', for creating me.

List of persons to whom you are thankful.

1.
2.
3.
4.
5.
6.
7.
8.

...and so on...

Make a list of things and blessings for which you are thankful.

1.
2.
3.
4.
5.
6.
7.
8.

Chapter 5

POSITIVITY IN LIFE... YOUR ATTITUDE

Your health, destiny, social status, etc., all depend upon your positivity. How positive you are in life decides your attitude towards life. Positive thoughts bring good health, wealth, happiness, love and bliss to your life. The positive person is very close to oneself and to the creator as positive thoughts are life giving love enhancing and health improving. A positive attitude towards life can take you all the way to the top positions. Whatever may be the biggest aim that you have thought of, it can be attained through positive thinking.

Everything is possible with positive thoughts and positivity of the mind. Your mind is full of love, bliss and happiness. Your subconscious mind is the builder of your destiny, body and mind. It's on its job each and every moment of your life. You cannot interfere with its life giving pattern with negative thinking. Watch your thoughts as they flow out of your mind. Always remember, what the conscious mind is feeling, the subconscious mind is receiving and making impressions of. The beauty is within you.

When you share something with someone wholeheartedly, you feel happy, pleasured and contented, even though it might be the tiniest thing. These are the positive thoughts in your life that make you happy. Today's positive thoughts shape your world and keep a record of your milestones on the path of your destiny. They set the goals you want to achieve in your life. Negative thoughts take you away from all these beautiful and life-giving options. It's your life and you decide what you choose. Whether you want to show yourself as sick, feeble, impatient and immature in front of others, it's your own choice. You can invite such negative thoughts into your mind anytime and can add as many bad things in your life with your negativity

Try to be positive so that this energy attracts other positive things for you in your life. Life is full of choices. Feel good for yourself and the rest will automatically become good and positive. If you think positively for yourself and negatively for others, you are again on the wrong frequency. The negative thoughts will dominate and harm you with more strength than the person for whom you are emitting those negative thoughts in the first place. The ultimate loss will be your own. Positive thoughts will take you closer to the creator, the universe, and the supreme soul. Each of your thoughts has a frequency. When you send out a thought in the universe, message with the same frequency come back to you, whether positive or negative.

Here is an interesting story. A child of about seven years was once sent to stay in a boarding school. His parents periodically went to his boarding school to meet him. He visited them too whenever he had his vacations. Everything was going well until he attainted the age of fourteen. At that time, he was in ninth standard. One day, his parents received a message from his school that he had been suspended from the school as well as the hostel for two weeks, and that they could take him home for this period of time. The parents as well as the child found it difficult to face one another. The situation was awkward and the worst for the entire family.

Somehow, giving some explanations, the parents brought their child home. Then, they inquired him about several things. They asked him several questions as they wanted to know about his behaviour at school which had resulted in his suspension. The child was very sensitive. He kept on crying the whole day. His confidence level had come down a great extent. This is how the situation remained for three-four days. His parents were observing his behaviour and were feeling sorry for him. The child was in great mental agony.

Finally, the parents decided to bring their child out of that state of mind. Slowly, they started keeping him busy in the tasks which he liked the most from whenever he used to come home from his boarding school during vacations. His mother started taking care of all his needs and carefully chose her words while talking to him. She also started staying at home to spend more time with him, talking about his interests, likes and dislikes, while also sharing with him her own choices, likes and dislikes. This resulted in the development of a good equation between the child and the mother. She also started telling him stories from her childhood, her college days, and how she wanted to do a lot of things just like him.

The mother shared with her child the things that she used to feel when she was his age. Slowly, his father also started trying to be friendly with him. The child started trusting his parents. One day, he broke out and narrated to them each and every incident that happened back at his boarding school. The parents sat calmly down and listened to everything that their child had to say to them. From this conversation, the parents came to learn how much their child had suffered due to small incidents, and how he had been wrongly labeled as undisciplined and irresponsible. They also got the chance to learn how good their child actually was. He was full of values that all parents expect from their children at that age.

They also learnt that their child was greatly attached to them, and respect his parents as well as teachers equally, except for those one or two teachers who didn't understand him. He has a great liking for and bonding with his friends too. The child discussed all his problems with his parents. The period of suspension was passed by somehow. Now, the child had started analyzing things quite well between good and bad, had become more confident and wise, which proved him to be a very good boy. A suspension like that had come as a bad situation for the parents and the child, but a lot of positivity came out of it, as the child started trusting his parents from then on and started sharing all his problems with them.

Even the worst situations can leave a positive impact on your life. Never feel desperate when things are going wrong or against you. Those are actually meant to test your patience and see how positive you can remain in such a situation. Always be positive. Your life should be a guiding torch for yourself and others. Make 'being positive' a habit. Make it a lifestyle. Positive situations and happenings make you feel happy and teach you how to find happiness. On the other hand, negative situations can also teach you very positive and wonderful lessons that add to your personality and thoughts to become more positive. Remain happy, even if you are surrounded by negative people and the negative situations created by them. Even in the darkest night, you are able to see something, if not everything. You can feel something.

Whenever you find yourself in a very dark room, you always try to open your eyes wide to see. Then, you give your mind a chance to figure out where the door, the switch board, a candle, a matchstick or a torch is. If it's your own room or house or office, you are able to find these things easily, not with your eyes, but with the power of your mind. Thus, no matter how bad the situation may be, it can leave a positive impact on your life. Be a guiding star, not a mocking spectator standing in a big crowd.

Always walk ahead with positivity; let the world follow you. Create the positive attitude within yourself. Speak positive words. When your mind, whether conscious or subconscious, emits positive vibrations, they come to you, as many more minds and souls are on the same frequency. Whatever vibrations you let out in the universe, come back to you. When you look back on the dark side of your life again and again, you also go back to your past and think about the disappointments and miseries you suffered at that time. As a result, you attract those disappointments and miseries for your future also. Instead of attracting negative things in your life continuously, you need to give it a pause and move forward.

Try to collect thoughts of happiness, bliss, peace and thankfulness, i.e., all the positive powers of the universe. When you accumulate these positive powers with positive thoughts, you fill your life with joy, happiness, success, good health and wealth. Don't create ill luck for yourself by being negative in your life. Life is full of choices; choose the best for yourself. You are not born to live in negativity or poverty. Happiness, success, good health and wealth are your right. Create your destiny with positive thoughts which will attract all the positive things in your life.

'*You are the designer of your destiny. You are the author. You write the story. The pen is in your hand and the outcome is whatever you choose.*'–Lisa Nichols.

Focus on whatever you want in your life. Start from today itself. Put a full stop on your past. Take your past failures as real life lessons, don't mock them. Those were your first hand experiences. Learn from those experiences. Start acting on them right away. Create a beautiful positive world for yourself, visualize, and most importantly, start working on them right away. Positive actions on your part will make your dreams come true.

When you want to achieve something and you use your positive energy for it, the entire universe comes into action to make it possible for you and helps you in achieving that, no matter how. *How* is not your concern;

let the universe decide it for you. You just pray, how the prayers become true is not your concern. You must have observed that all life coaches teach us to focus on positive thinking and develop a positive attitude, because without this you cannot have a positive life. If the mind is full of negativity, you cannot even think of a positive life.

Life is full of choices; it's up to you what you can choose for yourself. Every bad situation gives you two options, i.e., positive and negative. It depends upon you what you want to choose for yourself. Face every negative situation with a positive attitude. Positivity in life has the potential to change everything. Positivity brings more success and achievements in your life. Your ultimate goal is to stay healthy, wealthy, successful, happy, peaceful and blissful. This can only be possible with a positive attitude. One negative thought can spoil your entire day, sometimes even waste days, weeks, months or even years of your life. Whereas, one positive thought can make your day and fill you with a new positive energy to work and chase your dreams with a renewed zest and zeal.

Make your enemies your friends if that does not change their mind, your attitude will confuse them and one day, you will feel that they have also changed and become friendly towards you. Positive words have a great force. Don't say even a single word of negativity to anybody, because if you have been positive to them for a long time, that one negative word will wash away all the trust that your positivity has built up between them and you.

Always be positive to yourself and approach other positive persons. Create positivity in your mind. If your conscious mind is positive, it will give the same positive information to your subconscious mind as well. Your subconscious mind cannot differentiate between the real and the imaginary, between good or bad. Thus, when you give only positive thoughts to your mind, the subconscious will only pick that positivity. With a positive attitude, you can cross all hurdles of life to reach the top. Love thyself, act with a positive attitude -and success will be yours.

Always keep this in your mind, 'My life has a purpose and so does yours. We are all here to make a contribution that is uniquely ours. We all have our parts to play in this drama of life. You can turn your life around from wherever you are .No matter where you start from you can always change your circumstances for the better.'

Check your mind every day. Am I really upset today, or did I expect more out of that situation? Take something positive out of even the worst situations .Choosing to be positive and having a grateful attitude determines your way of living life. Your attitude determines your personality positive minds leave the steps behind them to follow, negative minds leave nothing but agony and despair, your life is a blank paper–scribble the words of your choice.

Exercise 5

Check your mind for how positive you are!

Imagine that it's raining today. You feel great pleasure to know how it's watering the earth, plants, buildings and everything else around you. The cool breeze makes you happy. Now, if this doesn't interrupt your routine job, it is positivity. While if you feel distracted and want to sit free at home without going to work, even if it is very important for you to finish your work, it is a negative thought. Make a list of such occasions when you have been positive and negative.

Make these lists under two separate headings, and ask yourself,' Why was I not positive at that time?'

Positive reactions:

1.
2.
3.
4.
5.
6.
7.
8.

Negative reactions:

1.
2.
3.
4.
5.
6.
7.

Chapter 6

CARING AND SHARING

"Caring about people, about things, about life is an act of maturity."

–Tracy McMillan

Caring and sharing–these two words are very closely knitted. Sometimes, you share your belongings only with those whom you care for, but this does not always happen. Some people are so caring that even the problems of people unknown to them disturb them and they rush to help them without a second thought. On the other hand, there are such persons who never care for anyone.

Caring and sharing teach you how to share your belongings with others. Sometimes, you even share your things with those who are not your family or friends or related to you in any manner. You do that because you feel that those people really need your attention help or they are deprived of certain things which you have in ample.

Adding a caring attitude to your life makes it smoother. You can then make a long list of persons who really feel good about you. Your gestures are appreciated, which add value for you in the caring and sharing account of your personality's bank. A person is known for his deeds, not for his looks. Make it a habit to donate to a needful person. If you don't have any money to donate, donate your good wishes. Make your own account of feelings, put good wishes in it for everyone, and one day you will feel yourself the richest person on earth.

When you care for one, you get many more caring hands too .Measure the people around you with the beauty of your heart as well their not the wealth. The color of skin of people around the world may be different, but the basic structure of one's head and body–two eyes, two ears, one nose, one mouth, two hands and two legs is the same. Emotions and feelings are controlled by the heart and the mind together. Bring the best out of it. These are the steps towards the achievement of bliss, peace and a successful life.

Here is a beautiful story. Two friends were once sitting in a small restaurant in the country side. They saw a man sitting on the next table. He filled a glass of water, then a second, and then a third, then drank all of them one after the other. From his appearance, he seemed as if he hadn't eaten for many days. One of the friends thought of giving him something to eat, so they called for the waiter and ordered for the man in rags along with their own order. The restaurant boy served him with a plate of two sandwiches. The man in rags looked at the boy, who in turn pointed to the two friends sitting at the next table. The man in rags looked at them, but without acknowledgement.

As he picked up the first sandwich, a little girl–also in rags–walked up to him and stood next to his table. The man gave her a sandwich, which she ate hungrily. He then picked up the second one and handed it to the girl too. She grabbed it and ran away. He pushed away the empty plate on his table, filled up a glass of water again and drank it. He then stood up and walked out of the restaurant without a backward glance. The two friends were really moved by his selfless act of generosity.

When you share your things, they come back to you in abundance. The things you share are not limited to your material possessions. You can share your knowledge, ideas and views as well. Helping and caring hands are better than praying hands. Mother Teresa cared for the sick and ailing people, despite the difference in their nationalities and race. She spread the message of love, care and sharing throughout the world. In beautiful worlds, she said, "If you can't feed a hundred people, then feed just one."

Extend your two caring hands many more caring hands will come to join you. Start with your journey of care from this very moment. Help a person, care for a patient, or a depressed and unhappy person. When you care for someone, you feel a strong inclination to share your belongings with that person. Some people care for the humanity at large. Someone has said, "When you really care about people, their happiness starts mattering to you more than your own." The person who cares for and shares with the humanity at large, has so much love for humans that no matter who and where they are, they immediately start thinking of ways to help them.

Love is the purest feeling. Habits of caring and sharing are the outcome of love. Such habits are also the result of positive upbringing. In many schools all over the world, the concept of caring and sharing is taught as a subject in the form of moral studies. Not only this, one full week is celebrated in this regard where the children bring surplus items from their homes or a little amount of money from their parents to contribute in the name of care and share. This week is also known as the 'joy of giving' week. Children are encouraged to donate small essential commodities to those who are badly in need of them. Those collected articles and money are then donated to the particular groups that work for the benefit of orphans, the old aged, ailing, helpless, deserted people, etc. Sometimes, such contributions are made to the victims of natural calamities such as a famine, flood, tsunami, draught, etc.

The world is full of generous people. Every person has one's own unique definition of caring and sharing. Many times, people regularly put a little share of their money in donation boxes which are meant to help the underprivileged who deserve their help. A caring and sharing attitude is a high quality of your nature and should be a part of your behavior, but it should not be practiced at the cost of your own 'self'. Care for all those who care for you. It is not possible to share everything, but sharing a little money once in a month or a good piece of advice to those who really deserve it is good practice.

The medical and paramedical staff cares for their patients, parents care for their children without any expectations, and you care for your friends and relatives. In today's world, people donate their eyes to the blind the other organs to those in need of them, and blood to help the ailing in their treatment. Many philanthropists run organisations to make the underprivileged members of the society meet their ends.

Life is full of challenges .When you care for someone without expecting anything in turn many such caring hands join you in this journey. Both caring and sharing should be done sensibly. Sharing the wrong things can lead to pain and does not help anybody in the long run. Care and share without expectations. Expectations lead to disappointments. Selfless caring and sharing automatically adds to your satisfaction and increases the level of your success. It's very important to keep in mind to do acts of kindness and then forget them. Many people call it wrong, but if you donate a little portion of your money and essential commodities to those who really need it, you can't expect them to give back the same to you. Thus, help without expecting. Share happily and unconditionally. Virtue is its own reward.

Caring and sharing is another step forward to a successful, happy, blissful, healthy and wealthy life. Care from the core of your heart. Think of those persons who have cared for you in the past and are still caring for you in the present. Always remember those who have ever helped you when you were in a dire need of them. It will strengthen your power of caring and sharing, and these people will play as role models in your life. Nourish your mind to care for yourself and the others. Share your belongings so that they can multiply and fulfill the needs of others.

You are the wisest creation of the Creator on this earth. Share your love with all other beings. If you don't share your happiness and love with the others it will not be multiplied. Care for others so that the others care for you too. If parents wouldn't share their affection with their children, the latter would never learn what bonding is. If teachers wouldn't share their knowledge with the world, it would remain illiterate. If nature itself wouldn't spread its message of love, care and share in the form of the cool breeze, rays of the sun, protection of the mountains, the nourishing plantations and all other creations, there would be no world at all. Caring and sharing gives you a lot of happiness.

Exercise 6

Make three lists for this chapter. First of all, make a list of all the persons who have ever helped you by caring about you and sharing their belongings with you.

1.
2.
3.
4.
5.
6.
7.
8.

Make a list of those whom you have helped.

1.
2.
3.
4.
5.
6.
7.
8.

Cross out the list of those whom you have helped. It's not an important list. The most important list is of the persons who have helped you.

Make a list of those persons who could care for you and help you, but never showed up. For example : Your parents

1.
2.
3.
4.
5.
6.
7.
8.

This third list is very important as it gives you the inspiration to not to refuse help and care to those whom you are capable of helping.

Chapter 7

SMILE, AS MUCH AS YOU CAN

"Let us always meet each other with a smile. Smile is the beginning of love,"

- Mother Teresa.

Smile, the tiny movement of your lips, can make your face beautiful, peaceful and blissful. Smile enhances the beauty of the face. A beautiful smile can change your life as well as the life of whosoever comes in contact with you. The journey of smiling starts from the very birth of a child .No doubt, all infants cry at the time of birth which is essential for their health as it supplies oxygen to their brain ,but the child's first smile makes the parents, relatives and their friends smile too. Their faces glow with the same eternal smile as the baby's. When this child grows up become a mature adult, he forgets to smile somewhere along this journey.

Smiling is the art that costs nothing. Anybody can develop this art and make their life easy and beautiful. Even when you are not very happy from your heart, or have great sadness in your life, you can still try to smile so that the others feel that you are giving off positive vibrations. Smiling faces have the force to change the most stubborn, jealous or even criminal minds. A person with a pleasing personality is always remembered. He leaves a long-lasting impression on the minds of others. But here, the smile should be innocent, from the depth of your pure heart, and one that reflects your positive and original mind. It should be without biases and away from any vices or guile.

Win the hearts of people without hurting them mentally or physically. Your positive smile has the force to change the atmosphere around you. If a stubborn boss changes his mind and starts greeting his employees with a smile each morning, his changed attitude will inspire a new energy in his employees to work .The biggest enemy of a person is his own mind, his own negative thoughts. Analyse every thought that comes to your mind, forget and overlook the negative things with the smile.

Here is a beautiful story. One day, the employees of a big company reached their office and found a big sign on the door, saying that the person who had been hindering their growth in the company had passed away. All the employees were invited to a funeral arranged in a big hall. There was a coffin placed at the centre and all the employees gathered around it. In the beginning, all of them were sad to hear about the death of one of their colleagues, but their curiosity soon grew to find out who in the company itself was this person who tried to hinder the growth of his colleagues. After much deliberation and excitement, they decided to see who it was. Everyone thought, 'Who could it be that was hindering my progress? Well, at least he died!'

One by one, the employees approached the coffin and looked into it. They were speechless. They stood shocked near the coffin and were all in deep silence. There was a mirror inside the coffin. Upon seeing their own image in the coffin, the employees were all spell bound. Next to the mirror inside the coffin, it was written, 'There is only one person who is capable of setting the limits of your growth, and that's you!"

Your life does not change when your boss changes, or when your company changes, or when your location changes. Your life changes only when you change it, when you go beyond your limiting beliefs. So, smile and examine yourself. Face the difficulties, challenges, impossibilities and losses head-on. Be a winner, build yourself and shape your destiny. It's the way you face life that makes all the difference. A smile lightens our mind from every problem. It is like a ray of light coming from the sun into a dark room. It purifies our mind, soul and body. Smiling faces are beautiful and heavenly.

When you visit a hotel in any country, the staff welcomes you with a smile .Although that smile might not be from their heart it still creates an aura of beauty and happiness. Similarly, when you board a flight or alight from it, the crew welcomes and sees you off with a smile. The smiles on their faces make you feel happy and confident. If you add this smile to your life dealings too, more smiles, more happiness and bliss will start coming into your life. Always smile from your heart. It conveys the message that you are good at heart, happy and helpful.

Two neighbours Emily and Jane, were very good friends. They both had maid servants at their respective houses. One of them had a young maid at her place while the other had an older woman as her domestic help. Jane's family members kindly referred to her as 'Aunt'. Emily, on the other hand, shouted at her maid servant all the time. As soon as the timid girl would enter the house, Emily would lift the entire house on her head. She would shout very meanly at the poor girl. Emily tried to get her household tasks finished quickly and neatly, without calculating how much time it would take a normal person to finish the same work. Emily's house was full of confusion the whole day.

On the other hand, Emily's neighbor, Jane, was a calm lady. Emily was surprised to see that their helper aunt was perfect in her work and Jane never needed to shout at her. One day, Emily went to Jane's house. It was Christmas day and she found that Jane was giving away cloths, food and other household articles to aunt with a graceful smile on her face. Aunt was also very thankful to Jane. Emily went to Jane's house on other occasions too when 'the maid aunt' was there, as she was keen to know the secret behind the peace in their house. Emily found that Jane was instructing aunt to do various tasks around the house in a very polite manner and with a smile on her face. Whenever the aunt did something wrong, Jane would calmly instruct her to correct it. Jane also helped the aunt's children with the books they needed for their studies.

Emily grew wiser with the passage of time and learned Jane's secret. She tried to inculcate in herself this practice of smiling, which resulted in a great change in her behavior in the long run. Emily shifted from that house to a new place, but she remained Jane's friend. One day, she found out that Jane was battling cancer and had been admitted to a nearby hospital. Emily decided to go see her and throughout the way, she kept thinking that Jane must be in great pain, and would probably be very uncomfortable and crying. But to her utter surprise, when she reached Jane's room in the hospital, she saw a bald lady with a beautiful smile on her face, lying in her bed.

Jane immediately recognized Emily and said, "Emily, you are here to see me! I'm so happy."

Emily said with tears with her eyes, "Jane, I was unable to recognize you. You look so different. Are you alright?"

Jane replied with a smile, "Yes, I am .Due to this young doctor, I am alive."She pointed towards the doctor, a very handsome, tall, and young man who entered the room and bowed to Emily in a manner of wishing her. With a little effort, Emily recognized the young doctor and uttered with surprise, "You're aunt's son, aren't you? Are you a doctor here? What a pleasant surprise!"

Jane said, "He is the reason behind my smile. I'm alive because of him. Even in such great pain, he never lets me feel low."

Emily now truly understood Jane's smiling behavior with others. Her behavior brought people closer to her even when struggling with such a dreadful and painful disease, due to the calm smile on her face. The secret is that a smile has the power to change the mind of even the cruelest person. Smiling faces are full of beauty, bliss and happiness. Laughter is indeed the best medicine.

A very pleasant saying by Danis Waitley–"A smile is the light in your window that tells others that there is a caring, sharing person inside".

Exercise 7

Make a list of persons who made you smile today, yesterday or the day before yesterday.

1.
2.
3.
4.
5.
6.
7.
8.

To how many faces were you able to bring a smile today, yesterday or the day before yesterday? If none, try to bring a smile to at least one face daily. Write down the list of such persons.

1.
2.
3.
4.
5.
6.
7.
8.

Chapter 8

NOTHING CAN STOP YOU

Our life is like the flowing water. It crosses every hurdle that comes in its path; it crosses the mountains, rocks, huge stones, cuts the layers of earth, flow through cities, states, countries, continents, etc, but remains true to its nature. When the water stops flowing and stands there for a long time, it stagnates, pollutes itself and the nearby places. Keep up the wheel of your life moving like water to make it meaningful for yourself and others. The wheel of time is moving fast don't let your life stop.

No one can stop you from achieving big. You and you only, are your biggest enemy. Before starting anything, you often decide for yourself, "I can't do it, it's so difficult…!" Such notions are only hindering your path .Instead, convey yourself, "I can do it. It's not at all difficult, but an easy job…!" When your mind starts taking the thing like this, your path will become easier.

In the previous chapter, I presented an anecdote of how employees of a company all collected together for the funeral of a colleague who had been creating hindrance in their growth. After seeing themselves in the mirror inside the coffin, they came to know that no one else was a hindrance in their path except for themselves. Their negative thoughts were the only hindrance in their path.

Everybody is busy creating his/her own destiny. You have to create yours without criticizing others. Try to appreciate the efforts of others in your life. Think of all the people who have ever helped you. Don't miss even a single person, not even the one who once carried your bag for you, or gave you a glass of water when you needed it, or had given you a good piece of advice.

Any work done with attention, focus and positivity never goes to waste. Try to develop the skill of being positive and you will feel that nothing can stop you. You might have misconceptions in your mind that somebody is stopping you from doing certain things. The fault is in you, or in your way of taking or visualizing things.

"Our greatest weakness lies in giving up. The most certain way to succeed is always to try just one more time."–Thomas Edison.

A young couple once moved to a new neighborhood. The next morning while they were having breakfast, the young woman noticed that her neighbor had hung out some washed clothes but the clothes were not very clean. She said to her husband, "She doesn't know how to wash clothes properly. I think she needs a better detergent." Her husband remained silent. Every time the neighbor would hang out her washed clothes to dry, the young woman would comment like this. This went on for a month.

One day, she was very happy to see that the hung out clothes of her neighbor were very clean and sparkling neat. She said to her husband, "Finally, she has learnt to wash clothes properly." The husband said, "I got up early in the morning and wiped clean the windows of our house." The wife understood the truth. She had now come to know that it was not the neighbors' clothes that were dirty, but their own window panes. So is life.

Before criticizing others, you should check your own state of mind. A mind burdened with negative thoughts takes on things heavily, negatively and in a fault finding way. You can't even take a break to think positively. Your thought process works throughout the day; it is a never ending activity. What your mind thinks, it starts feeling like that too. Our thoughts, whether good or bad, positive or negative, go to our subconscious mind which innocently starts working on them right away. If you start nourishing and feeding negative thoughts in your mind, it'll only give you negative results and negative things will start happening in your life.

If you water good thoughts, good things will happen in your life. This positivity will be all around. Thus, the universal law of attraction is absolute. Positivity begets the positive and negativity begets the negative. Negativity or negative thoughts affect oneself more than any other person. Negative thoughts create mood swings, feelings of dejection, unwantedness, loneliness, depression, and affect your health, both mental and physical, in the long run.

In your growth and your path of success, you have to be very stubborn and move with a positive mind. Each and every vibe of positivity will come back to you. Failures are important in life; they teach you how to be a stronger person. Falling is not bad. If you fall, rise. Fall again, rise again and go on like this because it will strengthen your mind and determination. When you fall, you rise up with double the force. Nothing can stop you, make your focus clear.

Clean your mind and put positive thoughts in it. Tell yourself that you have the ability to do anything. You must say to yourself, "I am capable of doing this work. I am the best person to do this and my Creator has created me to do this." Every night is followed by day and every day ends in night. But darkness is always followed by light. Take your mind towards the brighter side of your life. During this journey, if anything negative, sad, or unwanted comes into your life, its impact will be less on you. You will immediately become stable and start your journey towards success again.

All things cast shadows when light falls on them. Every person has a shadow when standing in the light. That shadow follows you everywhere you go. The choice is yours whether you want to hold on to that shadow, or move forward to your success. It's a universal law that whatever is thrown toward the sky will come back down towards the earth due to its gravitational pull. Similarly, the type of thoughts you give out through your spoken words, feelings, etc., with the force of your mind, will come back to you with a similar force.

Inculcate good values within yourself, and they will result in positive thoughts. Only positive thoughts can take you towards success. Keeping in mind this fact that nothing can stop you, you should walk onwards on your journey of success. Think, ''Why has the Creator created a human being like me? What was His need to create me?" Try to think positively and you will get the beautiful answers. Try to value yourself and time, so that the others will also value your presence and time will recognize you.

Exercise 8

Set a target then fix a time limit for it. Work in the direction to achieve your target with positivity.

Make a list of events which have been left incomplete due to your own negative thoughts, when you felt that you couldn't do something.

1.

2.

3.

4.

5.

6.

7.

8.

Change this list into positive actions that you can do to realize your goal. Nothing can stop you, nobody can stop you.

1.

2.

3.

4.

5.

6.

7.

8.

Chapter 9

ACCEPTANCE

"The first step toward change is awareness. The second step is acceptance." – Nathaniel Branden.

Acceptance has two forms; one is acceptance of the self, while the second is acceptance of others as they are. Accept yourself as you are–good or bad. Accept yourself whether you are overweight or underweight or have a low self-esteem. Despite of various faults in your habits or personality – accept yourself as you are. Accept the conditions as they are. It will make you own up to the responsibility of your deeds that have resulted in a low self-esteem or any other such fault. Acceptance of the self gives you the chance to move on from it and improve yourself on the journey of lifelong success. The more you accept the reality of life, the closer you will get to a successful life. Life is a journey. As when travelling from one place to another, your mind accepts the physicality of your travelling encounters, of what comes after what, since your imagination cannot come into play here and you accept the things as they are. But what you need to change is your own perceptions.

To be closer to life, happiness and fulfillment one need to accept all human beings as they are .Every time you have a choice whether to help someone or not, just give and give without any expectations in return. Accept your friends, relatives, fellow beings as they are. You cannot change anyone of them. Instead, you need to change your vision and way of perceiving the situation. If anybody has been harsh with you in the past, just put yourself in their situation and you will realize that you too could have reacted in the same manner in that situation.

You always expect from the people around you to accept you as you are. Normally, you don't change yourself .However, if you want to impress somebody, you momentarily try to change yourself according to that person, but the results are still zero. It is because the person for whom you are changing yourself is not capable enough to understand that you are trying to set yourself in his/her mould. The person will not understand your effort or sacrifice, as he himself is not ready to accept things as they are.

Sometimes, you get irritated or annoyed by others' behaviour and make up your mind regarding their qualities or label them as 'bad', but you never think of what you would do in the same condition. These people are not bound to act upon your dictates, so just accept them as they are. Here, when you start accepting people as they are, you will feel that they have also started accepting you as you are – without expecting any change in you.

In the journey of life, you may face many situations which you have to tackle. Every human being is created equal by the Almighty. Accept yourself as you are created by 'Him'. No matter if you have a short height, or are very tall, have a dark complexion or fair, wide or small features or whatever color your eyes are, just accept yourself as you are. The Creator has given you the best features that suit your face. You are one of the best creations of God.

Appearance does not make a difference; it is made by your attitude towards life. Helping people are liked and loved by all. Accept yourself, and the world will accept you. Inculcate the basic qualities in yourself that nature has given to every human being at birth. The qualities of a very small child are the basic qualities given to us by nature. It is when he doesn't know what is bad or how to cheat others. Innocence is the basic quality. Every soul is born with the qualities of love, purity, knowledge, peace, happiness, bliss, etc. Acceptance teaches you how to adjust with others. Right from birth, the child learns the qualities of adjustment, tolerance, confrontation, judging, withdrawing and discriminating. A child accepts his parents and siblings as they are when he is an infant, but when he grows up, he loses the grip of this power of acceptance because he starts pin-pointing the faults in others, their work, manner of speaking and behavior.

The same child has the power of tolerance, as he tolerates the behavior of his elders, whatever that may be. He faces the situations alone when he first steps into the school or boards a school bus or goes to play with other children in the playground, and accepts everybody there. He accepts the teachers, staff, students, drivers, conductors, peons, etc., as they are because as a child, he is closer to the quality of acceptance and feels himself closer to his parents and the Almighty as well.

After sometime, when he grows up and indulges in gossip and negotiation, he starts judging and discriminates them as per his choice. Life's journey is like this. Every situation leaves us with two thoughts – the thought of acceptance and the thought of denial. Here, you accept yourself, but don't force your acceptance over others. Even when you feel rejected by the whole world, you don't reject yourself. The goodness of your mind will always be there to accept you.

Accept your mistakes. Accept yourself as well as others as they are. Expecting others to accept you as you are is a sheer wastage of your talent, energy and time. Before going to bed every night, review your day's activities. Now, review the acceptance of various situations. All situations may not always be favorable, as a human has to face a variety of situations. Accept the situations as they are.

For example, if you go to somebody's funeral, you accept that his/her close relatives, friends, etc., are sad, and if you start laughing or giggling, no doubt the people there will doubt your state of mind, that the situation has not brought about any change in it. Here, you command your mind to accept that situation and behave like a normal and prudent person. Opposite to this, if you face a situation where all the persons present are happy, laughing and celebrating an event that gives them joy, but your state of mind is not well or you are sad about something, and you start crying ,people will doubt your state of mind even in that situation. Hence, accept the situations as they are because they cannot be changed immediately.

“Accept, then act .Whatever the present moment contains, accept it as if you have chosen it. Always work with it, not against it....this will miraculously transform your life.”–Eckhart Tolle.

This is also a fact: We cannot accept all the situations that come in our lives, but we can change our mood and feelings by not attaching too much value to them. Furthermore, don’t feel dejected in such situations. All bad situations will pass like a fast moving train or an aeroplane, as long as we don’t pay any attention to them. Like the other powers of your mind, acceptance is also one. The power of acceptance is a very mature quality of your mind. Accept the persons around you as they are for their different natures, behaviours, tastes, choice, etc. Accept the situations as they are. Martin Luther King Jr. has said in beautiful words, “The art of acceptance is the art of making someone who has just done a small favour wish that he might have done you a greater one.”

Exercise 9

Your power of acceptance can be checked by a small exercise. Make a list of persons whom you have accepted as they are.

1.

2.

3.

4.

5.

6.

7.

8.

Chapter 10

NEVER BE JUDGMENTAL

Humans have developed themselves over time. Their cranial capacities have increased over the years so have the feelings and thoughts towards one another; some good and some bad. One of them is the concept of judgment .Here I would quote a short fable to explain my point .The story is about collecting pieces.

An old man in a village didn't like his neighbor who was a young innocent boy .So he spread rumours about him that he is a thief. He was arrested by the police. After being arrested, the trail proved that he was innocent .After his release, he filed a defamation case against the old man. The judge heard both the parties and told the old man to write all the complaints against the young man on small pieces of paper and throw all the pieces of paper on the road while on his way back home. The old man agreed. The judge told him that he has to collect all those pieces scattered on the road and bring those to the court at the next hearing. The man was astonished and said that it was impossible to do so. The judge's point of view was proved. The old man learnt a great lesson that one should not judge people and spread rumors about them unnecessarily.

Many a times you judge a person without getting to know the reality. Before speaking ill of others, it is very important to investigate the matter.

Once, a rich man's son met with an accident. He needed immediate surgery. The rich man repeatedly shouted at the hospital staff to call the doctor immediately, since he was not in the hospital at that time. The hospital staff was trying its best to give the child first aid and prepare him for surgery, but the rich man continued to shout at them, "Why is the doctor so late? Is he so irresponsible? How far is his house?"

In the meantime the doctor reached the hospital. As soon as the father saw him, he grabbed him by his collar and started shouting, "Why are you so late? My son's life is in danger." The doctor went inside the operation theatre without replying. It took him three and a half hours to perform the surgery. When the doctor came out, he informed the rich man, "Your son is completely alright. His surgery was successful, don't worry!"

The rich man who had been annoyed, arrogant and abusive sometime back, tried to express his gratitude to the doctor now, but the doctor didn't even pay attention to what he was saying and left the place without saying another word. The rich man asked the hospital staff, "What sort of a man is this doctor?" The entire staff remained silent. He asked again, "When I held his collar in anguish, he was calm. Now when I wanted to thank him, he rushed away!"

One of the staff members, an old nurse, answered with tears in her eyes, "His son died yesterday in a road accident. He was at his burial when we called him for your son's surgery. Now that he has saved your son's life, he is rushing back to finish his son's burial." The rich man was shocked and ashamed of his behavior. He was unable to utter even a single word.

One should never judge anyone, because you never know how their life is or what they are going through.

On many occasions, you rush through things on account of having to go somewhere .In this process, you end up delaying many other persons because you judge yourself to be better than them. Every person has his own abilities and disabilities, but you often judge a person rashly.

Once, a middle aged couple was going to attend a very famous person's lecture in their town. While on their way, they saw a car trying to overtake them again and again, but they did not allow it to do so. The wife said, "Drive faster or we'll miss this very important lecture. Don't let that car overtake you." The husband started driving very fast, when all of sudden, a tyre of their car burst and it skidded sideways. The occupants of the car behind witnessed the whole incident and immediately stopped to help the couple. They changed the tyre of the car, took the couple to a nearby hospital since they had suffered minor injuries, then one of them left the place hurriedly.

After sometime, the couple was discharged from the hospital and they decided to attend the lecture anyway, even though they had gotten a little late due to the small accident. When they reached the venue, they found that a large crowd had come to attend the lecture. The hall was completely silent as the lecture was going on and they could only stand in the last row to watch.

The husband was astonished to notice that the person who was delivering the lecture was the same guy who had been driving the car behind him, trying to overtake him, and who took them to the hospital and helped change their car's tyre after the accident. He told his wife, "Look, it is the same man who helped us. We were unnecessarily scolding him for overtaking us. Now I understand why he was in hurry."

The wife felt ashamed of herself for having insisted on her husband to not allow the car behind him to overtake. Now they realized that thousands of people had been waiting for his lecture, but nobody was waiting for them. Despite his busy schedule, he helped them before going to the venue to deliver the lecture. The husband uttered, "How good the person is!"

Don't be judgmental .Everybody is running their own race. You cannot judge a person from his looks, clothes or situations .Try to accept them as they are. Sometimes, you cannot judge a person by his deeds even, or by his appearance.

Emily, as a young girl, was told by her mother that men and women sitting by the riverside are not good human beings. In reality, those people were fishermen and fisherwomen. Emily's mother advised her not to go there alone, but she was very curious to know why her mother had said so .One day, she went there along with her friend Jenny, without the knowledge of her mother .She saw that those men and women were fishing and selling the fish to customers. Emily was confused why her mother had told her that they are not good people.

She started going there along with her friend everyday without the knowledge of her mother. One day, when they were playing, Jenny accidentally slipped and fell into the river. Emily was frightened. She ran back home and narrated the entire incident to her mother. First, her mother was angry to know about her disobedience, but then she rushed to the place to help Jenny along with Emily. When they reached there, they found that one of the fisherwomen was carrying Jenny in her arms, and her clothes were wet. The other women were also helping her in different ways. Jenny was saved. Emily and her mother were very thankful to the fishermen folk for saving Jenny's life. Emily's mother also said sorry to her daughter about her misconceptions regarding the fishermen folk. Emily's mother learnt the truth that never be judgemental and that nobody can be judged by his appearance or his profession.

You cannot judge a person by his appearance alone. Behind a simple look may lie a lot potential and unexpected talent that can turn governments and invent ground-breaking modern machinery. Don't ever make up your mind about others until and unless you actually understand and know them. Sometimes, you cannot come to know about the skills of others in one or two meetings. In their initial meetings, many persons may not be very impressive, but later on can prove themselves, the best. The famous Indian freedom fighter and philosopher, Mohandas Karamchand Gandhi, popularly known as Mahatma Gandhi–father of the Indian nation always dressed up in hand woven cloth around his loins. He visited many countries of the world, wearing only his loincloth, and was able to compel the Britishers to leave India. If he had been judged by his attire only the story of Indian independence would have been very different.

Exercise 10

This is a very important exercise. You cannot build your opinions about others without properly getting to know them. The behavior of a particular person in a particular situation is not sufficient enough to judge him. Make a list of persons whom you have ever judged and have been proven wrong about it.

1.
2.
3.
4.
5.
6.
7.
8.

Also make a list of occasions when you were right, but were judged wrong and it hurt you a lot.

1.
2.
3.
4.
5.
6.
7.
8.

Cross them out one by one as you try to understand the situation of those whom you have judged wrongly, and how hurt they must have felt by your behavior.

Chapter 11

HABITS CAN BE CHANGED

It's an old saying that habits cannot be changed. In some language there is a proverb that says – Habits of a person end with his life. They remain the same throughout a person's life. But habits can actually be changed with little practice and a strong determination .In his book titled 'The Power Of Habit', Charles Duhigg introduces us with the scientific study of habits. One must have thought, "What does the word 'habit' actually mean?" It is a behavior pattern acquired by frequent repetition or physiological exposure that shows itself in regularity or an increased facility of performance. In simple words, 'habit' is doing something repeatedly.

Sometimes, we observe that a person is in the habit of tapping his fingers on the table, biting his nails or lips, rolling his eyes without a reason, or shaking his legs, etc. Many people are in the habit of taking a nap after lunch, or a stroll after dinner. Habits vary from person to person. Almost all human beings have some same habits, but the habits that spoil your social image and are not good for your personality are really bad habits.

A habit is a particular setup of your conscious mind fed into your sub-conscious mind. Sometimes, our bad habits tarnish our social image.

Once an officer, about forty years of age, was transferred to a new office. He was in the habit of blinking his eyes too often. Whoever came to his office to get a file signed or for some other task, would witness this odd habit of his. His female co-workers start feeling that he was wrongfully flirting with them. Almost all of them began to gossip about his behavior. Finally, they discussed the problem with their male co-workers, and they all started noticing his behavior. In the meantime, the male co-workers suggested to the female co-workers to not visit the cabin of the boss. Even when summoned, the female co-workers would not go into his office. Finally, it reached the boss's ears that all the co-workers were hesitant to come to his office.

One day, the boss finally called for a meeting. All the male co-workers came to attend it, but the females were still absent. The boss asked them, "Why has the female staff not come?" One of the male co-workers courageously answered, "You blink eyes at them." The boss understood the reason behind the unrest in his office. He soon decided to change his habit of blinking his eyes too much. For this, he took the help of his wife and children. With a strong determination, he was able to change his habit.

Habits can be changed, no matter how old they are. If you adopt good habits in life, they will not harm you, your family or the society. On the other hand, bad habits harm you and damage your social image at large. Bad habits should be short lived. As soon as you become aware of your bad habit, you should try to change them. What does it take to change one's habit? It costs nothing .You simply have to observe yourself and try to leave that bad habit with the help of proper counseling or reasoning in your mind.

A student was in the habit of skipping school on the pretexts of stomachaches, headaches, toothaches or aches anywhere in his body. Due to this habit of his, he grew weaker in his studies, he was short on the lectures attended, and was unable to cope with the syllabus. His parents were very worried about his aches and illnesses, and took him to doctors repeatedly. The teachers were also becoming irritable as he was not up to the mark with his attendance or in his studies. They often gave him piles of notebooks of other students to take down notes for missed classes.

Soon, the matter reached the school counselor. She was a very intelligent and wise lady. She asked the student, "Do you really think you have a headache, stomachache, backache, toothache, or any other ache which you complain about?" The boy and his parents were equally astonished at this question, but the boy replied shyly, "Today, I only have a headache, no other pain."

The school counselor then took out a paper from the drawer and wrote 'headache' on it. She showed the same to the student and his parents then tore the sheet into two. Then, she opened a second drawer and took out a 'star badge' to put on the boy's shirt's pocket. She told him, "Today, you are the winner since one of your enemies, 'headache', has died. Thereafter, she asked him and his parents to come to school again the next day to meet her again

When they returned the next day, the school counselor asked, "What's troubling you today?" The student said, "Backache."The school counselor repeated the exercise from the previous day and rewarded him with another star while declaring him a winner again. She repeated the same exercise for the next ten days. The student started coming to school with all those 'star badges' on the pocket of his shirt. When the other students asked him what were those badges for, he told them proudly, "I'm a winner. I have changed my habit of not coming to school."

With the help of the school counselor thus, the student changed his habit and started thinking of himself as the winner. Not only did he become a regular student he also turned out to be the best student.

All habits can be changed with a little cffort and observation. Habits are the product of both our conscious and the subconscious mind. With a little effort, even the oldest habits can be changed. When any bad habit starts getting set in your lifestyle, your way of talking, or treating others, etc., you need to change it. Meditation is the best way to change even the hardest and oldest of habits like alcoholism, smoking, wandering, etc.

For shedding off a bad habit, you first have to set its pros and cons. Make a list of merits and de-merits. Bad habits often cost you your health, for example, a person in the habit of taking alcohol, drugs, or smoking should make a list of the benefits and damages of such addictive practices, then compare what loss you have suffered in relationships due to these habits. What has the monetary loss been like? How many friends have you lost? Your confidence level must also have come down.

As such, habits can be changed with a little effort. For leaving bad habits and adopting good habits, you need to train your mind. You need a few days' practice, depending upon your will-power and self-discipline. Take a week or a fortnight to replace an old bad habit with a good one. You can embrace good habits any time.

Exercise 11

List out your bad habits, or the habits which have made you suffer.

1.

2.

3.

4.

5.

6.

7.

8.

Try to change your habits. Work on one habit at a time. Fix a time limit to change it. After changing one write a short note on how you worked upon it, how long it took to change it, etc. Develop new and better habits in their place.

Chapter 12

BELIEVE IN YOURSELF

Believe in yourself, or else nobody else will believe in you. Every person is full of capabilities and competence to do many things. Even those born with mental or physical disabilities have a lot of potential in them to do many tasks. A few days back, I was watching a reality show on television where I saw a girl, about twenty years of age, performing a dance with only one leg. I was so impressed by her that I started feeling that most of us human beings with two legs and all the rest of our body parts intact are doing nothing better with our lives.

You have taken birth here for a reason. Every human being is here on earth for a reason. It's up to you to find a valid and solid reason for your presence on planet earth. Ask yourself, "Why has the Creator created a creature like me? What was the necessity?" Start believing in yourself and your abilities. You have the capacity to move the hardest rock. If you believe in yourself, only then will the others believe in you too. Believing in the Almighty will make you stronger. One's strong beliefs in one's capacity make one successful in all spheres of life.

The former President of India, Late Mr. A.P.J. Abdul Kalam once said, "Never believe in what the lines on your hand predict about your future. People who don't have hands also have a future..."

Tell yourself that you have the capacity to do whatever you want to do. "Believe in yourself! Have faith in your abilities! Without a humble but reasonable confidence in your own powers, you cannot be successful or happy," said Norman Vincent Peale. Self confidence is to believe in yourself and your abilities to do some work.

Your focus is also important to achieve your target. Focus is a part of the belief that you can do the task in your hand and can achieve your target with constant hard work, devotion and faith in yourself and the Supreme. The law of nature is absolute. The sort of vibrations that you sent out into the universe, come back to you sooner or later. The words you utter, ill or soft, travel through the universe and come back to you to leave an impact on your life. Like a bullet shot from a gun, or an arrow shot from a bow, though they never come back, but their impact falls on your life.

In the famous Hindu religious epic, the 'Ramayana', King Dashratha shoots an arrow from his bow in the direction of a sound, assuming it to be an animal drinking water from the lake, but the arrow strikes the only son of a couple, Shravana, who was taking his old and blind parents on a pilgrimage. The last words uttered by the old parents of Shravana echoed in King Dashratha's mind for the rest of his life, ultimately resulting in his ill-health and death. Ill words uttered can never be pulled back, so don't speak even if you don't like someone or the situation. Silence is better than many ill-spoken words. The ill-words affect not only the person to whom they are uttered, rather the entire universe. They pollute the environment and the atmosphere around you.

Once there was an old man who used to say offensive words to all the passersby. People avoided going from the path where the old man used to sit or stand. His presence was a nuisance for everybody. Some teased him as mad, while the others ignored him as being old and feeble. One day, a person was passing by the way where the old man used to sit. To his astonishment, the old man was calm, not uttering a single word, rather busy doing something. He went closer to the old man with the intention to check whether he was the same old man or somebody else sitting in his place. But it was indeed the same old man.

He went back to his village saying, "Come and look! The old man is silent. He is not scolding anybody anymore!"The village people came running in numbers asking, "What? Why? Is he alive? What's wrong with him? Is he well?"Wanted to confirm with their own eyes, all the villagers went to see him and check on his state of mind, but the old man was stable and happy. A wise man among the villagers who dared to talk to the old man asked him, "Sir, may I ask you something?"

"Yes," said the old man without looking at the wise man. "Are you all right, sir? We just wanted to know about your changed behavior," the wise man uttered deeply and sighed.

The old man looked deep into the eyes of the wise man and said, "I understand now that the truth of believing in the self is more important. I used to rebuke everyone, thinking that people will come to me and respect me, but...nobody liked me. To seek their attention, I abused almost everybody who visited this way. I have changed my ways and now know that when you believe in yourself, other people will also start believing in you and will come to you themselves. Prior to this, nobody ever came to inquire about my health and well being."He continued with eager eyes, "I have learnt the great truth of this nature. I have no need to attract anybody anymore. People will come to me of their own and talk to me." The wise man was spellbound upon hearing these words. He was astonished by the secret told by the old man.

Believing in yourself is more important than knowing whether others believe in you or not. When you start believing in yourself more effectively at the time of setting a goal and making positive efforts to achieve it, you will be successful very soon. For that, you'll have to once look back at your past achievements, no matter how big or small they may be. Even the smallest achievement matters.

If you secured very good grades in 10^{th}or 12^{th}standard, or if you won a race at school, or even secured the second or third position, it is an achievement no matter the colour of your medal. Likewise, if you cooked four different dishes in two hours, or served food to ten people at home without any help or made a class project to which the entire class clapped for you, it is an achievement. Think about the applause, about the appreciation by your parents, family, friends and guests to whom you served the food. You attained these little achievements while believing in yourself. These achievements from the past, no matter how small or big, make you happy and strengthen your belief in yourself.

Once you've set a target, just think about it, live for it, do every positive act towards it, all while believing in yourself. No matter what the target is, you will be successful in achieving it one day. Positivity is very important. A single negative thought can take you back a whole step. In order to believe in yourself, start your journey with self confidence. Talk to yourself daily, "I can do it…I can do it…" Nothing is out of your reach. The strength of your mind and positive thoughts will make things easier for you and add to your journey of success.

Believe in yourself wholeheartedly. Tell yourself with full confidence that the Almighty has chosen you to do this task, and nobody besides you can do it more perfectly and accurately. The law of nature is perfect and absolute. What you believe in comes back to you. So, believe in yourself for all the positive things. You can achieve whatever you want to achieve in your life. Put your thoughts into practice. If you dream of something, try to achieve it. Self discipline is very important for that. Change the channel of your thoughts as quickly and easily as you are able to change channels on your television to find one that suits you the best.

Your thoughts attract those things to you which you believe are yours. As you emit the frequency of achieving something, the law of nature starts working on it automatically. Believing involves various activities like thinking, speaking and acting as if you already have those things in your life which you want. When you give out the frequency of wanting something, the law of attraction moves people, events and circumstances in your favour so that you receive it. Start believing that you are already in that position, or imagine receiving that thing wholeheartedly.

In his book 'Transformation: You'll See It When You Believe It', Wayne Dyer professes that when you begin to believe in your success, you will see actual results in your life as well. When you begin to believe in your ability to reach your goals, you'll see your beliefs manifest on a physical plane. Keep doing the things. Start believing in yourself. Rehearsal is very important. Your subconscious mind does not know what is 'real' and what 'imaginary'. It cannot differentiate between the two. Tell yourself daily that you are successful and that you have achieved your goal. Feel the situation, visualize it, and live it daily. Your subconscious mind is very strong. It will make it happen one day.

Exercise 12

On how many occasions have you believed in yourself and worked with full confidence and been proved successful. Make a list of such occasions to strengthen your self-confidence.

1.

2.

3.

4.

5.

6.

7.

8.

Chapter 13

PAIN IS INEVITABLE, BUT SUFFERING IS OPTIONAL

Pain, whether mental or physical makes you feel deeply hurt. The intensity of pain felt depends upon person to person and their response to the pain. Some people feel less pain and some more in the same situation. Pain is always seen on one's face, but sometimes some people have such a strong bent of mind or great tolerance power that they are able to curtain their experience of pain. Many a times we observe people crying with pain, while the others might just remain calm. It depends upon the choice and the mental setup of a person regarding the feeling of pain.

Similarly in the winter season some feel more cold while some feel it less. Some people can even be seen shivering due to the cold, whereas the others are not bothered by the weather at all, despite wearing nothing more than just a thin cardigan. During summer time likewise, many people can be seen sweating profusely, while the others are comfortable with the same intensity of the weather. All depends upon one's setup of the mind. Right from childhood, your elders teach you that fire is extremely hot and it burns everything, while ice is extremely cold and it numbs your hand. In general practice, both fire and ice have the same impact, as fed into your mind since your childhood.

You can train your mind to deal with any intensity of pain. You must have seen or heard of people walking on burning coals. No doubt, they have the same impact on their feet as any other person, but their capacity to bear that pain is different. Similarly, the country's soldiers who are posted at the borders high up in the mountains covered in snow and glaciers, experience their hands, feet and often their whole body freezing and rotting, but inspite of that they never cry out of pain. They have been psychologically trained to face such type of pains and to remain calm in such situations. Their mental condition and perception protect them from severe pain.

There once was a hardcore criminal whom the court had granted a death sentence. Now, it was the duty of the state and the cops to execute the sentence. The police cops, in consultation with the doctors, decided that instead of passing electric current though the convict's body to cause his death, they would perform a different psychological experiment on him. They tied the convict up in a chair and told him that they had decided to give him a poisonous cobra bite instead of an electric shock to cause his death. What the doctors and the police cops had planned was to only prick him with a needle, and not an actual cobra bite.

According to their plan, the doctor asked the convict, "Are you ready for the cobra bite?" Crying bitterly, he uttered, "Yes."He had no option since the death sentence had already been passed. He knew that his death was certain, this way or that so he consented in a feeble voice. He was blindfolded with a black cloth and the doctor pricked him on his palm with a sterilized sewing needle. The convict shouted and started behaving as if he had indeed been bitten by a poisonous cobra snake. He was shaking and his body started turning blue, as if the snake's venom was indeed travelling through his whole body.

All the police personnel and doctors were astonished to see how his body was reacting. The convict had turned blue and spit was coming out of his mouth. He died within a few seconds. When the post mortem was done, the doctors were surprised to find that his body was full of poison, as if a cobra had actually bitten him. They examined the needle with which the prick was given, but it did not have any trace of snake venom on it. The psychologist then determined that as soon as the convict received the prick of the needle, he mistook it for a cobra's bite and his body started making poison on its own. The reaction had been so fast that it took his life.

Thus, the phenomena of pain work from the mind. When you are in pain, your neurological system starts working and the nerves immediately send a message to the brain that there is pain in some particular part of the body. Thereafter, you start behaving accordingly. The convict in the above story did not die of actual physical pain. Rather, he died of mental agony. If you experience pain in your body, you have to face it and undergo it. If you are suffering from the pain of an ailment, you can reduce the intensity of that pain through positive thoughts. Suffering is optional, it depends upon your mind how you react in a particular situation.

It's all in your hands. Suffering is a choice. If you hold on to positivity in such situations, sufferings cannot come near you. Become a judge for your own self, what do you want to choose–suffering or happiness? You are not in pain or unhappy because of the deeds of others. If you are sad, unhappy or suffering it is because of your own thoughts. Become a pure soul as it was sent by the supreme when you were born. As a child, you never experienced a lot of suffering .Whenever you cried in pain, a soothing touch by your mother lessened it. Start feeling about the same stage again. The supreme, your universal father, gives you his invisible hand to sooth your pain.

The origin of all pain and suffering is in your own mind. Sometimes, you must have tears rolling down your cheeks, despite there being no bodily pain or an instance of getting hurt by anybody. This is because you created a thought in your mind that today you are sad, lonely, tired, feeble or unable to do work. You are in a sad mood, as if you have been deprived of the whole world, even though there is no reason for it. It is simply your own perspective that hurts you and makes you cry bitterly. Thus, all the suffering and pain starts from your own mind.

In the olden days, when anaesthesia was not available, surgical operations were conducted without giving any sedation to the patients. People had to bear all the pain caused by cuts and stitches, but in those days too, the experience of pain varied from person to person.

Psychologists once carried out another experiment. Five men, almost of the same age, were made to sit in a dark room tied to five different chairs. The team of psychologists told them that they were going to be taught emergency landing protocol in case of an aircraft break down. For that, the psychologists told them that they would be made to board an aircraft, and then be moved out over a slide to save their lives during an emergency landing. At the same time, they conveyed to them that their eyes will remain blindfolded during the whole process, but there would be no danger to their lives in this exercise.

After taking their consent, the experiment began. The five men were tied to five different chairs, as if their seat-belts were being fastened in an aircraft. They were blindfolded and headphones were placed over their ears. An announcement was made by one of the trainers, that they were now taking them to the aircraft. They started rolling their chairs around the hall to create the delusion. Certain sounds were played in the room and through their headphones to make each of the five men believe that they were travelling in an aircraft. After one hour, an announcement was made that they need to make an emergency landing, which meant that they had to save themselves.

They were made to descend from a nine foot high wooden slide. While sliding, all of them displayed different pain reactions. All five of them fell over a cushioned floor, but the trainers told them that they had fallen on soft land. While they were sliding, they were fearful their faces were pale with pain, agony and confusion. All of them were crying and shouting loudly.

The objective of the experiment had been to see how much pain one feels while sliding out of an aircraft in case of an emergency landing. It was also observed that all the five men complained of severe pain in their joints. The entire effect on the body of these participants had been psychological, not real. The participants in fact hadn't even been taken out of the hall where the experiment began.

The blindfold was removed from over their eyes and all of them found that they were in the same room where they had originally been made to sit. On inquiring, they came to know that they had not been taken anywhere. The entire one and a half hour long experiment had been administered in that single room only.

Pain is a natural reaction which you learn through the various practices of a pure mind. Some of you must have learnt in your childhood that if you fall from a moving cycle, it will hurt you. A slap on a cheek is painful, but more than the physical pain, it is insulting. The pain felt during an operation is less, but the post operative pain feels greater since the patient knows that there are cuts and stitches on his body from the surgery.

Pain is as you feel. Some experience less pain or no pain, while some experience a lot of pain. Its intensity depends upon your state of mind in a particular situation. How one reacts to pain is an individual's matter. Some people know how to manage pain, as its effect varies from person to person. Some people are more hurt upon seeing the suffering of others. Your heart is full of pain when you see a child bleeding. For a moment, you forget your own pain, even if you are bleeding too. Thus, pain is inevitable, but suffering is optional.

"If you can smile when you feel hurt, the hurt is half cured," says Ruskin Bond.

Exercise 13

No doubt, pain is inevitable, but suffering is a choice.

Make a list of occasions when you felt pain in your body, but you felt it less. List also the events when people conveyed to you that a particular situation will make you sadder, but you remained calm and bore the feeling of pain well.

1.

2.

3.

4.

5.

6.

7.

Chapter 14

THE REAL HAPPINESS

All human beings are in search of real happiness and in that quest, they choose many paths.

The definition of a journey towards real happiness in life differs from person to person. What is real happiness? Have you ever thought about it? Is it earning a lot of wealth? Or spending a good time at a beach without any worldly stress? Does playing with waves count for happiness? Or spending time with your family or friends or dear ones? The tasks and activities done with a positive mind and with good vibes make you stress-free and take you towards happiness. Some people find their happiness in their family, a few in work, more in health, some in doing something good which is of their choice, or in following their hobby or dream, or in achieving their goal.

You must have seen that the people who have earned a lot have faded, feeble, pale and unattractive faces. They make themselves look attractive with makeup and such things. If wealth had the power to make you happy, the wealthiest person in the world would be the happiest too. But that is far from reality. Wealth is an essential part of life–bless it, keep it, share it, spend it and help others with it–that is the true sense of happiness.

When you help a person who is in need of money, it is a moment of real happiness for that person who has received your money. Happiness can be generated inside you through your deeds and in good thinking. Happiness is the product of your own mind. The meaning of happiness varies from person to person.

A rich lady visited a counselor once, in search of happiness. The counselor called in Anna, who used to clean the floor of her office. The counselor said to the rich lady, "I am going to ask Anna to tell you the secret of her happiness and where she found it? I want you to listen to her carefully." Anna put her broom and mop on the floor, settled herself in a chair and started narrating her story. She said, "My husband died of cancer and three months later, my only son got killed in a car accident. I had nobody – nothing was left for me. I couldn't sleep. I couldn't eat. I never smiled at anyone. I even thought of taking my own life. Then one day, when I was returning from work, a little kitten followed me home. I felt sorry for the kitten as it was very cold outside, so I decided to let the kitten in. I gave it some milk and it licked the plate clean. Then, it purred and rubbed against my leg. I was receiving affection for the first time in months. I smiled and paused to think that if helping a little kitten could make me smile, perhaps doing things for people would make me happy. So the next day, I baked some biscuits and took them to a neighbor who was sick and in bed. Every day, I tried to do something nice for someone. It made me so happy to see them happy. Today, I don't know of anybody who sleeps or eats better than I do. I have found my happiness in giving to others."

When the rich lady heard the story, she started crying. She had everything that money could buy, but had lost the things that money could not buy. The beauty of life does not depend upon how endowed you are, but how happy others are because of you. It has been said, "Happiness is not a destination, it's a journey. Happiness is not tomorrow, it's now. Happiness is not a dependency, it's a decision. Happiness is what you are, not what you have."

Do the tasks that make you happy. Happiness is a decision to remain happy. A well dressed old man, aged 92 years, whose wife had recently died, moved to an old aged home. The boy there who was escorting him described the room to him on their way. He told the old man, "Sir, there is your room. A sheet is hung there, which is to serve the purpose of a curtain. There is a small table which you can use to keep your things... "and so on the boy went on describing the room to him. The old man interrupted him and said with the enthusiasm of a ten years' old boy, "I like it very much." The boy was astonished to hear the old man's words, how he had determined that he liked it without having even seen it. He said, "Sir, you haven't seen the room yet. Hang on a moment, we are almost there."

"That has nothing to do with it," the old man replied."Happiness is something I choose in advance. I have already decided to remain happy," he continued, "I always thank heavens for those parts of my body that are still in working order. Every day is a gift given to me when I open my eyes in the morning. I focus on the new day and all the happy memories that I have built up during my life." He further said, "Old age is like a bank account from which you can withdraw only later in life, but have gone on depositing in along the way. I advise you to deposit all the happiness you can in the bank account of your memories."The old man then thanked the boy for his part in filling his account with happy memories and told him his simple guidelines for happiness.

1. Live simply
2. Give more
3. Expect less
4. Free your mind from worry
5. Remain away from hatred

Always keep in your mind that happiness is a choice. You must have heard someone saying, "I cannot remain happy for too long, as sadness always follows or something wrong happens." No doubt, each day is followed by night and each night turns into day and this natural system goes on. But sadness is not forever. Even in the hardest and the worst situations, there is always a ray of hope. Happiness is merely a choice. When you choose to be happy, no outside disturbance of the mind can affect you. Deposit the best memories in your brain's account so that whenever you feel sad or low, a happy moment from your past can immediately pull you out of that mood and boost your morale.

If you know the real value of happiness, only then can you remain happy or make the others who are attached to you happy. Accept all things happily. Give as much as you can without any expectations. Your happiness does not depend upon the decisions of others. Real happiness is when you accept all your relations, good or bad, as they are. Accept those too who expect you to change as per their wishes. You often need to change your vision towards life to become happier. The happiest are those who make others happy. Happiness is a lifelong process. Collect, pick and choose the happiest moments of your life and keep them safe in the locker of your heart. Open it and bring out the happiness joined to them whenever you feel that your life has become sad.

Some people feel that they will be happy if they earn more money. If money could buy happiness, no rich person would ever be deprived of it. Happiness is an internal feeling which you choose for yourself. Even a penniless boy performing little jiggles on the roadside to earn his piece of bread for the day could be happier than a person who is struggling to earn more and more wealth. Happiness has a real meaning for that boy, i.e., to make others happy with his small tricks. No matter if he is doing so to earn some money for himself, he is doing his job with full satisfaction and happiness to make others happy.

Happiness begins with small things. A small achievement can make you happy. Your help to someone else makes you as well as the other person happy. Give more happiness to others, and you will receive more happiness back. Happiness is when your heart is full of joy. Make each and every moment of your life the happiest. Enjoy the present with your full heart. Happiness is in your way of thinking and your vision towards life. Real happiness is long lasting and stays with you forever.

Exercise 14

Think about the situations of your past when you were really happy and contended. Make a list of such occasions.

1.

2.

3.

4.

5.

6.

7.

8.

Chapter 15

LOVE - THE UNIVERSAL COMPASSION

No one is deprived of love in this world. One may think that no one loves them, but the reality is that everyone is loved or cared for by someone, whether one feels it or not. Here is a story of a little girl, named Elisa.

She was born to working parents who were very ambitious in their life. The child's birth was no doubt a cause of happiness for them, but her upbringing was difficult and challenging for them, because she didn't fit anywhere in their daily routine. Thus, her birth was a hindrance in their routine life and work. For this reason, the couple decided to send the child to her grandparents' place. She was loved and cared for a lot there, and got all the happiness of her life. The house was full of aunts and uncles. Moreover, she was the only small child in the house and was pampered by all the members of the family. When the child was about 3-4 years old, she was brought back by her parents to their house. At this stage, they were more concerned about her studies, health, well being, social status, etc.

At her parents' house, she now had a little brother too who loved her a lot.

The little girl, Elisa, thoroughly enjoyed the company of her younger brother. She used to play and quarrel with him all the time. Her younger brother was her entire life. The brother and sister shared a great bond between them. No doubt her parents were taking care of her, but in a very hurried manner, which she was unable to understand as a child. The girl grew up to become a young woman. Through all those years, she was always sad because she missed her grandparents, aunts and uncles. They had been her first childhood love. During all these years, she realised that she had never been loved by her mother, who always preferred her brother over her. Her father was often busy with his work, but he cared for her. Then, she got married to a man of her choice, rather the best man in the world who loved and cared for her. She was blessed with two wonderful children. The little girl, Elisa, was never away from love. Love had always come to her life in different ways and forms by means of different people, but the acceptance in her mind towards love was less.

We are all loved and cared for by someone or the other who makes our life beautiful and worth living. We often lose their attention because of our own behavior. First of all, start loving and caring for yourself. A child should take care of his studies, diet, etc., for the sake of his parents, which will ultimately help that child in the long run. A parent should first and foremost love and care for oneself. Only then can they take care of and love their children and help them become successful, loveable, and responsible in their life. Love for God, your children, parents, fellow beings, nation, nature, etc., make you different from the crowd. Those who love God become religious or spiritual in one way or the other. The genuine love of parents for their children in the form of positive guidance can make them lead a happy, prosperous and successful life. They, in turn, lay the foundation of a positive and healthy society. Love for your fellow beings leads to universal brotherhood. Love for the nation makes you a patriot and a healthy and responsible citizen. Love for nature makes you preserve nature in all its forms. Love is not a feeling that's only inside you, it's felt worldwide.

Love is a perfect universal force. To be successful in your life, love yourself. Whatever you attract comes to you; this is the universal law. Love is the supreme power of life. Give love through your good feelings. Love all those things that you want to have as a part of your life. Love for children attracts children towards you. If you go to a playground to see your children, and play and talk to them with affection, more children will get attracted to you. Love for nature attracts nature towards you. If you are enjoying nature in a botanical park and are loving the plants and flowers there, they will also seem to love you back. You experience a bonding with them and feel like going there every day. You love the aura of that place; it's celestial. The cool breeze touches your face and makes you feel closer to nature. You feel the heavenly feelings on earth; it is the most relaxing moment for you. When you love your country and say a beautiful slogan on a national festival, people seem to love you as they recite that slogan many times after you. When you love food, you'll get more and more opportunities to eat the food that you love to eat. When you love a certain kind of clothes, you will find the same type of clothes available in the market, no matter whether they are old fashioned or not launched yet. When you love to read books to satisfy your unquenchable longing for them, you will feel that love back from a number of books that are waiting to be read by you. Love attracts everything that you love.

You must have heard people saying that they love certain kinds of chocolates, fruits, food items, cakes, etc. Such people know of all the brands that make these things. They even know from where they can get them from all around the world. They know their origins too. Thus, the things that you love start coming to you. When a person loves travelling to places, he explores the different places that he can go to. Love builds a deep bond between father and mother, parents and children, children and their grandparents, between siblings, cousins, friends, relatives and between a husband and wife.

Love is the purest feeling, untouched by conditions. Parents love their children unconditionally. Similarly, God loves you unconditionally, as you should love Him unconditionally. Love is the basis of every relationship. Joint families, the society, a state and a country are all founded on the notion of love. Love forms the basic structure of the universe. With it, you can make your whole life, even your destiny. If you love money, you will find different ways to earn it. You will feel that money is also desperate to come to you. You will get a number of opportunities to earn more and more. If you love fame and start working in that direction, fame will also be eager to come to you. Never feel deserted; all things respond to the power of love. Love for mountains, along with courage, practice and self discipline can enable you to climb the highest mountain.

Love your passion. Prem Lata Aggarwal, a 48 years old Indian woman became the oldest Indian woman to scale Mount Everest. Her love and passion for mountains enabled her to climb the highest mountain peak. Johanna Quaas, a German female gymnast aged 91, has such great love for gymnastics that her name was entered in the Guinness Book of World Records for being the oldest performing gymnast. Your love for any game, goal or destination will definitely take you there, no matter how many hindrances there may be in your path. An Indian woman named Man Kaur, aged 101 years, broke the Guinness Book of World Record in javelin. She was the oldest competitor at the World Masters Games which is open to all athletes of all abilities. Her love for her game keeps her making records even today.

No doubt, I am writing this book for all age groups. Here, I have mentioned the two women to inspire you to keep going and enjoy your journey till the end of your life. The people who exhaust their passion after years of continuous success and hard work leave their passion and become sad and depressed. But then there are those who continuously love their passion and keep on moving throughout their life, even with the dignity of their titles. No matter how many times they lose, the ultimate success is in their hands. They are the winners of everything. The success is theirs. Hence, love whatever you have in your life. Love that too, which is not in your life. Love all the things which you actually want to have in your life.

Love is the ultimate force. It is the universal compassion that brings happiness, power, health, bliss, knowledge and wealth to your life. Love for the Almighty makes everything possible for you. You are capable of writing your own destiny by the power of love. You love whatever you want to get in your life. When the frequency of love travels, all the universal forces start creating circumstances to bring that thing to you. You should not be concerned with the 'how' of your fulfillment of wishes. It's all in the hands of the force that will create everything for you. Love with a pure heart, and it will bring you everything that belongs to you. True and pure love has the force to move the biggest of rocks.

When your heart is full of love, you will feel love for all the creations of the Almighty. You will never feel like hurting them. Every creation of God has a force of love. As like poles attract, people will get attracted by the force of love. Love is a power which overlooks the mistakes of others. Love yourself first of all, only then will you be able to love others. Love surrounds everything around you. Love your appearance, as the Almighty has created you. Love takes us closer to the Almighty. You must have heard people saying that they are afraid of God, or they are God-fearing persons. Here, you have to take a deep breath and ask yourself, "Has God ever asked anybody to be afraid of him?"He wants 'love' only. Love is the only emotion which the Almighty wants from you, for Himself and for his creatures.

Love whatever you have in life. Loving makes it easy to get things. Your love should be for the positive things in life. Your subconscious mind is unable to distinguish between the real and the imaginary. When your conscious mind loves a thing, you will start living as if you already have that thing. Your subconscious mind will start believing it to be true and will do every effort to bring the same to you, so always love positive things. Always be conscious of your wishes and choose them very carefully, so that you get only the positive things in life.

Life is full of love. Spread it with the utmost care and with the purest of thoughts. They will bring more love into your life. Love your existence on earth, love your every breath, love your soul make it a pure soul that is always ready to help others. Pure love brings the most beautiful things into your life. The image of your beautiful heart that is full of love reflects on your face. Pure love is never deprived of bliss, happiness, health or wealth. Loving hearts have helping hands. Love is a heavenly feeling. Always feel that you are loved by yourself. You are your best friend, nobody loves you the way you love yourself. Don't depend on others to be loved or cared for. The first step should be your own. Love brings love into your life. Loving hearts are caring hearts. Love your ambitions and goals, and try to achieve them with hard work and focus. Love everything that you already have in your life. Love makes life simpler, more beautiful and modest.

'Spread love everywhere you go, let no one come to you without leaving happier,' said Mother Teresa.

Exercise 15

This exercise for 'love' is very interesting and simple. You only have to make a list of your loved ones. Include your children, parents, friends, etc.

1.
2.
3.
4.
5.
6.
7.
8.

Make a list of things that you love and want to have in your life, like happiness, peace, wealth, etc.

1.
2.
3.
4.
5.
6.
7.
8.

Both the lists may be long, so you can add more pages to it.

List your hobbies too.

1.

2.

3.

4.

5.

6.

7.

8.

As you open your mind and start exploring it, you will find that the list of things and people you love is unending.

Chapter 16

DREAM BIG, SET A GOAL

Whatever you want to become in life, dream it, visualize it. Live out the whole dream in your imagination. It has an immense power to bring these things that you dream closer to you and help you fulfill them. Great achievers are first great dreamers and big thinkers. Practice for achieving a goal. Set a small goal initially, dream for it, then visualize and live it as if your dream is already true. Let your imagination go wild. When you start imagining these things, your mind will start accepting them as true and feel as if it is real.

During an interview after the completion of fourteen hundred runs in a test cricket series, the Indian cricketing prodigy Sachin Tendulkar said, "Life is flat without a dream. I think it is really important to dream and then to chase those dreams. It is the dreaming that makes me work so hard". Dreams play a vital role in a human's life. All big personalities have been dreamers. It's very beautifully said by someone that dreams are not those that you have when you are asleep; dreams are those that don't let you sleep till they are fulfilled.

When you desire something, it originates in a dream. When your desire becomes very strong to get or achieve something, it makes you dream and forces you to think on it again and again. Socrates has said, "When your desire to achieve something is as intense as when you want air, you will achieve success." All inventions in this world are the results of dreams. All big personalities have dreams. To achieve them, they work in that direction and successfully add something new to the collective experience of the human race.

The Wright brothers dreamt of flying in the sky like birds. To put their dream into reality, they visualized it again and again, and worked in that direction. Action was taken, experiments were made, and finally the Wright brothers made their dream come true and a milestone for modern inventions of modern day airplanes particularly, was laid. Thomas Edison dreamt of a light bulb. He set his goal to invent it and worked hard over it. Edison tried two thousand different materials in search of the filament for a light bulb, but none worked. One day, his assistant complained, "All our work has been in vain, we have learned nothing." Edison replied, "Oh, we have come a long way and we have learnt a lot. We now know that there are two thousand elements that we cannot use to make a good light bulb." Even after that, Edison continued to work on the same project and eventually succeeded in inventing the bulb which benefitted the whole humankind.

To be successful in life, dream big, chase your dream. For that, you'll have to set a goal. Try learning to achieve goals from small assignments. Like in school, a science teacher gives an assignment to his students to finish a project within thirty days. Those thirty days are the time limit set by the teacher to complete the assignment, i.e., the deadline to submit that particular project or to face the consequences fixed by that teacher. All students, except one or two, submit their assignments within the timeframe.

You too need to set your goal and finish your assignments within the time that you have proposed for yourself. Set a time frame for each and every task of yours. If you have set a goal to read fifty pages of a book in a week, but you manage to read only thirty, don't worry. You are still close to your goal. Give yourself some more time to complete the remaining pages, while also adding a few more pages to it. Same as when you are making a painting on a canvas, set a goal, fix a time within which you should finish the painting. If you are close to finishing in the time frame that you've fixed, it means that you are close to your goal. Effort, action and hard work are important.

No one can become a millionaire in a day. For that, you'll have to dream it, visualize it, live it, and most importantly, you'll have to set a goal and work hard in that direction to achieve it. Time management is very important to achieve a goal. Fix a time for all your tasks. Don't postpone matters that are important for you to achieve your goal. Think positively and set to work. The time will be yours. It will be favourable to you. When you have a very strong desire to make a particular change and you start working in that direction with hard work and utmost sincerity, forces of the whole universe come into action and join hands with you to help achieve your goal.

Setting a target is step one to fulfill your dream. Action and effort in the right direction is very important. When you dream something big, assure your mind that you have the capability of doing it, no matter what the others around you say. Nobody else can recognize your potential better than you yourself, so don't get discouraged by small hindrances that come in your way of chasing and achieving your goal. Without goals, you are like a kite flying with a broken string in the sky. You're then destined to fall to the ground without going upwards. So, set a goal and have a strong desire to fulfill it. All your planning should be in that direction only. Program your mind for success. Repeat your goals to yourself again and again. This will make you more confident about what you want to become in life.

Say you want to become a doctor, repeat this idea in your mind again and again, and start working in that direction. You must tell yourself, "I want to be a doctor. I want to be a doctor."This will program your mind to achieve the goal. Visualization is also very important. Create pictures in your mind of what you want to become. Rehearse it again and again. Besides visualizing, you must also repeat those things in your conscious mind. It will program your sub-conscious mind to do all those things for you. You have to visualize the steps necessary to achieve your goals. Visualization takes you nearer to your goal, and ultimately you will be able to achieve them in a very short span of time.

Dreams are those that won't let you sleep. A dream is that which you think, imagine, and visualize while sitting, standing, eating or doing any other task until you fulfill it. All successful persons use this technique.

When I was young, I used to see my little brother give speeches while lying in bed. His behaviour used to surprise me a lot at that time, but now after thirty years, I realize that he was only practicing, visualizing and rehearsing the speeches that he now delivers with confidence today at various renowned institutions. Other people who saw him doing so when he was young considered him a day-dreamer, but he went on to become a successful person throughout his technique that he practiced.

Motivate yourself to chase your dreams. Do all those exercises in your conscious mind that are required to fulfill your dreams. Goals are achieved by hard work and visualization. Setting a goal is very important. Before proceeding towards the journey of your success, see everything positive and the negative things will automatically diminish. During the transformation of your soul on your journey towards success, you may fail many times, suffer many falls–like a child when he is learning how to walk–but you will perfect it at the end, as a child not only learns how to walk but also runs and makes himself capable to run a race. In the same manner, success will ultimately be yours. Don't lose confidence in yourself. No matter how hard it gets, with any number of hurdles coming your way, your focus must always remain on your goal, and you will be the winner.

An old Indian story goes how a king once punished one of his ministers to stand in a cold pond through a very cold winter night. In the morning, the king was surprised to find the minister hale and healthy, and asked him how he had managed to stand in such cold water throughout the night. The minister replied, 'Sir, the earthen lantern enabled me to stand in the chilly water throughout the night.'

'How?' asked the King.

The minister said, 'It's the faint light coming from it that motivated me to stand here, despite the wintery night." The King understood the answer of his wise minister.

To fulfill your goal, even a small incident can play a vital motivational role in your life. The swimmers who have swum across the English Channel fixed their goal to achieve the task within a particular time and made their hardest effort to achieve it. The athletes or players who break world records first visualize their success and live their dream in their mind. They put it in their conscious and sub-conscious mind as true, then, work upon them till the day it truly happens in their life. Your sub-conscious mind has all the power to make your dreams come true. You can achicvc any goal as long as you work hard for it, despite the usual hindrances. Remain focused on your goal. The universe will create all the opportunities and circumstances for you that'll lead you to be successful.

Exercise 16

Make a list of goals which you want to achieve in your life. Divide the list under two parts. List A and list B. In list A write down the small or big goals which you have achieved till date, and in list B, write about the goals which you have set up in your life but are yet to achieve. For achieving any goal, you have to make efforts in the right direction with devotion and hard work.

List A

1.

2.

3.

4.

5.

6.

7.

8.

List B

1.

2.

3.

4.

5.

6.

7.

8.

Chapter 17

SELF DISCIPLINE CREATE SELF CONFIDENCE

So far, you have come a long way working on yourself and exploring your journey towards success and change. Step by step, you are learning and expressing how small changes in your vision, thought, behaviour and perspective can lead to major changes in the self. You feel yourself completely changed and ready for any success. When you become successful, you will think back on your journey with pride and enjoy the real fruits of your success. However, sometimes achieving success does not always translate to remaining successful. For that, you will constantly have to keep a check on yourself. Self discipline is an important tool that can ensure you success forever.

You must have observed that everything in this universe follows a discipline.Every living being follows discipline too, we all know that. Even non-living things follow discipline. Here, we'll explore how important self-discipline is, and what is its role in our lives. All celestial bodies complete their rotations and revolutions as per the rules set by the laws of nature. All mechanical objects are driven by a particular mechanism as per their programming. Similarly, you need to program your mind that needs training and constant practice.

Before delivering a speech or performing an act on stage, a performer rehearses his role and words over and over again. Players also practice a lot before their final performance at a match. Not only human beings even birds and animals have self-discipline. A herd of sheep moves together over the pastures, mountains and valleys. They always follow the one that leads them all. Similarly at sunrise and sunset, flocks of birds fly together in a particular manner, going out in search of food or returning to their nests in the evening. They follow their body clock and maintain a discipline.

In one's day to day life, a human has to watch his or her own discipline. Hence self-discipline is an important quality to inculcate in one's nature. When you are a child, your parents teach many things in the name of discipline, your teachers teach you many important things in life, "How to move in a group, sit in the class, to do your tasks daily, etc."

All institutions have their norms which you have to follow while you are there. The society in which you live also has certain principles. Your religion, if you follow any, has boundaries too which each and every member belonging to it has to follow, whether one agrees to it or not. Every successful person is self-disciplined. All sectors, whether public or private, need their associates to be disciplined and work accordingly.

How you behave in a particular situation decides your level of self-discipline. Don't ever come under the influence of others. Try to evaluate, judge, discriminate, and decide, then proceed to choose the best for yourself. As you write your destiny, write with the utmost care and intelligence. It's your life. Choose the best for yourself, no matter how many times you fail in doing so. In short, self-discipline is the positive programming of one's mind to do some particular things in a particular manner and at a particular time.

All relationships remain close, understanding and forever with self-discipline. Everything in this world has limitations. If you expand your mind within those limitations, it will give you real happiness. Let your mind soar high in the sky. The universe is also waiting to help you, but first of all, help yourself without harming others. Self-discipline gives birth to the self-confidence. When you have already programmed your mind on how to react in a particular situation, it will become very easy for you to handle even the most terrible situations easily. You always face two types of situations, good and bad. You should never expect anything from anybody. Expectations are hurting.

When you approach somebody for the first time, you feel a little nervous since you don't know how that person will react. If you are self-disciplined enough, you are already prepared to face any type of situation, whether the meeting is formal or informal. Even if it turns out to be terrible, you will find something good and positive in it and the extent of hurt on your mind will be minimum. This will help you come out of the situation successfully, without hurting yourself.

Rising up in the morning and going to bed at night is your routine. All of us do it, but it's a form of self-discipline that we've learnt since birth. In simple words, the day is for us to work since the day-light is spread everywhere, while the night indicates that it is time for us to rest our body and prepare it to restart the work again that next day. When you discipline yourself, you fix a particular time to wake up in the morning and go to bed in the evening. Here, you have programmed your mind to do the acts within the limit of yourself, without creating any inconvenience to others.

While driving on the road, you observe all the traffic rules. You make up your mind and train yourself for those safety rules. You are well aware that those safety rules are for your own safety and the safety of others. If you don't program your mind for that and break any of those rules, you get fined or punished for it. That is a forceful action to make you a disciplined driver or pedestrian on the road. Similarly, you have to make and fix certain rules and regulations for your mind and behaviour.

In my previous chapters, I have mentioned that you should let your mind think as widely and broadly as possible, and let it explore the entire world. Here, I am not contradicting that idea. Rather, I just want to say, "Discipline your mind to the extent that it achieves everything you want, but not at the cost of causing harm to others."This is the journey towards success. If it is founded on the tears and curses of others you'll only become successful for a very short span of time. A success that is based on the sorrows of others will disappear soon. You will fall back to the ground as quickly as you had risen up in your success.

On the journey towards success and transformation of the self, you need to be self- disciplined. Think positively and start doing positive things in that direction. Your mind has unlimited ideas in it. Your brain has a wonderful memory. Your mind has a great storage system. You have limitless potential to work and achieve whatever you wish to achieve in your life. Organize your life, time and abilities. Use the power of the conscious mind to tell your subconscious mind about positive things.

Hardcore criminals are not criminals by birth. They only train their minds to be bad and work upon being more and more brutal, cruel, and inhuman towards others to create a sense of fear in their minds. To present themselves as the most cruel they keep on working on such negative thoughts. They make every effort to become more cruel by not giving this kind of thinking a break. When punished by law or put into prison, the councilors convey to them and train them to actually realize their mistakes. Only then do they see the reality of what they had done. There, they are taught self-discipline and their mind is programmed in a positive direction. Vocational, cultural, spiritual and moral teachings are given to them.

People with negative thoughts and qualities can never be successful in their life. Every person has two options in life before doing anything-good and bad. Daily, you face different situations where you have to choose whether to speak or not. If you sense that a particular statement of yours can hurt the person listening to you, don't say it. Silence is better than uttering useless words. Discipline of the mind increases self-confidence. You can pull yourself out of the worst situations with it. Self-discipline makes you responsible, caring, supportive, forward, more focused, gratuitous, positive, optimistic, mentally and physically healthy, spiritual, and brings you closer to the universe. Self-discipline further helps you inculcate the values of successful people. Life is precious. Start the journey of transformation of your soul right from this moment onwards. Try to value time, even a second, before it becomes the past. The present is moving fast, while the future is yet to come. Now is the time to act and add value to your life. Proceed gradually, step by step, as the programming of the conscious mind initially requires a little practice daily. This is your life discipline it–not for the others, but for yourself. As the graph of your values goes upwards, all the negativity and the bad things in your life will lower down and take you forward on the journey of success.

It does not matter how many times you smile in a day, but how many people smile because of you. Your opinions and ideas may not be welcomed by all, but a confident smile on your lips will show yourself-discipline and self-confidence, which will have a healing effect on other people. All our forces working for the welfare of the people, the military deployed at the borders, the navy and the air-force, the police force, fire-fighters across the country, all work with discipline and self-discipline.Don't ever hesitate from doing positive things. While programming your mind, make sure that it works in the set framework to give faster and immediate results. It's important to set up a time-table for yourself, for all your tasks.

You can think about love, but not lust; you can be envious, but don't hold hatred in your mind; have self respect, but not egoism. Self-discipline polishes your mind and soul. When your mind is disturbed, you hurt others with your actions, words and gestures. The negative thoughts are given by you, the same type of negative thoughts are received by you. Exchange of such type of emotions results in stained relationships. Discipline your mind and live a burden-free life. Self-discipline provides a frame for all your emotions and feelings. When you are right, you need not give any explanations to anyone. Move forward with your head held high, but not with a high-headedness. Do whatever you want to do. Follow your passion. Think the best for yourself and start acting in that direction with full confidence. Success will be yours. Self-confidence will take you to the heights which you have set for yourself, and perhaps far beyond your imagination too. Try to fulfill your dreams with hard work, self-confidence and self-discipline. Work for yourself and for the betterment of humanity. Your idea of serving is awaited by the world. Put it in action and move forward. Spread the awareness that you have and share it with the world. Think confidently, walk confidently, and act confidently. Self-discipline will make you more successful. Don't make fun of others; they are working according to their own mindset. Their dreams may be different, but they are also on the same frequency as you. Self-discipline teaches you to respect others, while working consistently for your own progress.Self discipline and self confidence will take you to being:

1. Successful
2. Focused
3. Composed
4. Progressive

5. Powerful
6. Self-controlled
7. A visionary
8. Optimistic
9. Positive
10. Efficient
11. Constructively productive

Exercise 17

For a disciplined life, make a planner. Fix a schedule. Divide your day into hours, including your sleeping and waking up hours. Fix a time for rising up early in the morning, say 6 a.m. or whichever time suits you. Fix your sleeping hours also. Fix the time for going to bed, say 11 p.m. or as per your convenience, but regulate your routine. Fix the hours for working, sleeping, eating, walking and the other important activities that make up your day. A time table, when followed daily, will make you self-disciplined. For a student, it is important to fix study hours also.

Time Table

6 a.m.

7 a.m.

8 a.m.

9 a.m.

10 a.m.

Till 11 p.m. at night.

Follow it religiously.

Chapter 18

FORGIVENESS, TOLERANCE, INDEPENDENCE

Forgiveness – An Important Game of the Mind

As young children, almost all of us were taught by our parents to forget the bad situations and forgive those who've ever hurt us. As we grow up, we forget this forgiveness mantra. I don't understand why we forget such values and damage our own personality as we grow up. You are a tomb- a powerful guiding star that gives positive vibrations. A mind full of grudges is like a bullock-cart loaded with heavy wooden logs, and driven by weak oxen. No doubt, the burden of grudges lowers down your potential to work. Think and move on in life.

A grudge feels like a constant itch in your heart. Whenever you sit alone, search deep within your heart. If you feel something itching and hurting, it is a grudge. A grudge never allows you to free your mind from guilt. It leads you farther away from self acceptance. Forget your past, move forward and forgive all those who have ever hurt you. Start from zero, from being down to earth, or this emotion will make you its slave. You are an independent person who has to work with pleasure and happiness.

Choose the best for you. Here, I mean choose the best emotions for yourself. If you think about yourself in that regard, you are not selfish at all. You have every right to direct, shape and live your life the way you want. If you search the dictionary for the meaning of forgiveness, it goes something like this: 'The act of forgiving someone or something, the attitude of someone who is willing to forgive other people.' Start this practice from yourself. First of all, forgive yourself. Free yourself of all kinds of guilt. Forget the hurt from the past. Forget the grudges. The only method of forgiveness is to forget the bad moments of your life. Then, forgive those who have ever hurt you, intentionally or unintentionally. Your expectations are big causes of hurt for yourself. Forget and don't ever hold any expectations from anyone.

Forgive the acts of others, believing them to be a part of their behavior. Working on others' personality is not your duty. You only need to work on yourself. Forgiveness is an important game of the mind. Play it emotionally, sensitively, intelligently and wisely. You can't change your way of thinking until and unless you replace your bad emotions with good ones. You have to work on your mind.

Let's see how this game is played. The word 'Sorry' is close to forgiveness. Often, when you do something wrong to someone, you say 'Sorry'. This single word gives relief to you and the listener. But what forgiveness actually is can be understood by this story:

Two friends were once walking through the desert. After some time, they had an argument and one friend slapped the other on his face. The one who got slapped was hurt, but he did not say even a single word in return. He wrote in the sand instead, "Today, my best friend slapped me on my face." After that, they kept walking until they found an oasis, where they decided to take a bath. The one who had been slapped got stuck in the mire and started drowning, but the friend who had slapped him, saved him. When he recovered from the drowning experience, he wrote on a stone, "Today, my best friend saved my life."

The friend, who had slapped and saved his best friend, asked him, "When I slapped and hurt you, you wrote the words in sand, but now you write it in stone, why is that?" The other friend replied, "When someone hurts us, we should write it in sand where the winds of forgiveness can erase it away, but when someone does something good for us, we must engrave it in stone, where no storms can ever erase it."

In this way, you will be able to forgive a person even if he has done the worst to you. Forget every hurt and you will automatically forgive the persons who have ever hurt you.

Here is a story of a small family. A boy was once born to a couple after ten years of marriage. One fine morning, when the boy was about three years of age, the husband found a medicine bottle open. He was getting late for work, so he asked his wife to cap the bottle and keep it in the cupboard. The mother, occupied in the kitchen, completely forgot to do that. While playing, the little boy went to grab the medicine bottle and consumed some pills from it. It happened to be a strong medicine meant only for adults to consume in small dosages.

When the child showed signs of poisoning, the mother took him to the hospital. Unfortunately, the child died there. The mother was shocked and shattered. She was terrified at the thought of facing her husband. When the grieving father came to the hospital and saw the dead child, he looked at his wife and uttered just four words to her, "I love you, darling," His unexpected reaction shows us his forgiving behavior, and how he did not blame his wife for what had happened. He understood that child was dead and could never be brought back to life. There was no point in finding fault with the mother, as she too had lost her only child. What she needed at that moment was consolation and empathy from her husband.

So, forget and forgive. Change your fault finding attitude and learn to be free from all types of grudges. This is a mind game. If you play it perfectly, you will be free from all malice and your mind will be purified.

Tolerance-A Virtue Worth Value

Tolerance is the other name for patience. To be patient in situations that elicit arrogance can solve many problems. As time is the best healer, tolerance and patience make you stronger in the face of sufferings in the long run. Tolerance is the ability to accept an experience and survive something harmful or unpleasant. Forgiveness increases your ability to tolerate.

Overlook the mistakes of others and accept them as they are. Forgive them from your heart, even if you have felt bad and hurt due to their behavior. Only how you behave is your responsibility, not others. You cannot blame others for your own short-temperedness. It's solely up to your state of mind how you react in a particular situation. Tolerance increases your level of patience. You cannot mould the world as per your desires, but if you have patience and tolerance for certain things, you become more acceptable and accommodating in your family, at your place of work and in the society at large.

In this fast moving world, nobody has the time to pay attention to the problems of others. But if you listen patiently to an aggrieved person, it will increase your tolerance power and lessen the misery of that person. Tolerance is power; its examples are in nature itself. The Earth bears the ferocious rays of the sun without losing its nature of tolerance. The ocean tolerates the intense waves in it. The mountains tolerate the wrath of high speed chilly winds and heavy snowfall.

When one's tolerance power increases, the person becomes more mature, and is able to think more rationally and independently. Thus, it is a step forward on your journey of transformation of the soul. You must have observed small children going to school. On their way, some children pick up stones, a few collect feathers, while some collect leaves. Your values are like these small collections made by children on their way to school. During the journey of your life, you pick up and collect the values of your choice. Tolerance is just another value which you can choose for yourself.

It's your life and you have every right to choose the values you wish to have in it. The people who enquire about your health are concerned about your well being. Remember them, as their small gesture makes your day. You must have experienced that you have a much lower tolerance power now than when you were a child. The reason behind this is that at that time, the values in you were pure and without any mixture. As you grow up, the words, “Why should I?” enter your life and threaten to spoil all the values that you have collected through your journey.

Thomas Elva Edison had a remarkable tolerance power. While looking for a filament when inventing the bulb, he failed two thousand times. Despite the resistance, however, he was ultimately able to succeed. Tolerance takes us onward on the passage of success. Don’t let the little words of distraction by others affect your mind. Just walk on your path with clarity in your mind and you will definitely be able to achieve the highest goal that you’ve set for yourself.

“The highest result of education is tolerance,” said Helen Keller.

Tolerance is the ability to accept people as they are. It is to accept the actions and views of others. When you agree with other people who have views different from your own, it is tolerance. “Tolerance is the greatest gift of the mind. It requires the same effort by the brain that it takes to balance oneself on a bicycle,” said Helen Keller. Tolerance teaches you to be tough, hard and strong in life.

Before winning medals in Olympics or on any other international platform, the players practice a lot of times with patience. Their bodies and minds learn to tolerate the harshness of the game and its rules, including both failure and success. Your tolerance power increases your patience. You need a lot of patience to attain your goals. The tolerance power of your mind leads you towards peace, blissfulness, happiness, health and wealth.

In many communities worldwide, yoga, dance and hard exercises are done to make the mind and body strong. Actually, these activities increase your tolerance. The tolerance power of your body, combined with meditation, increases your mind's tolerance power. Practicing and doing one thing again and again to achieve something is tolerance.

Independence- The Style of Self-Success

When your mind is free of all the negative thoughts and passivity, you are independent of all internal hindrances in your mind. In your journey towards success, many people may come and give you their free advice or suggest you options. Think well which advice or option can benefit you. Think independently, considering both their negative and positive aspects. You can also categorise them into three parts: 'Suits you', 'does not suit you', 'can be considered in a particular situation'.

Make your goal crystal clear to yourself and fix a time for it. Suppose you have to travel a hundred and fifty kilometers by car and you have fixed two and half hours' time to reach there. Then, when you start your journey, you find a lot of traffic on the road and it takes you three hours to reach there. Here, you are not too far away from your goal, since there were a few unavoidable hindrances in your journey. Still, it is great that you managed to complete the journey, even though half an hour later.

If you travel at a very less speed and complete that journey in five hours, double the time that you had fixed, even then it's okay. But if you never start your journey at all, you will always remain far away from your goal. Independence of the mind and thinking plays a vital role on your journey towards the improvement of self in transforming your soul. Independence of the mind does not mean that you are independent or free of all boundaries or limitations. Independence is more enjoyable when it is within a limitation. Your body has limitations. Your tongue has certain limitations too. You cannot utter rubbish and stupid words. Independence of the mind is to think rationally without hurting the emotions of others. Independence of the mind is when your mind thinks without the influence of others. You are free to develop your ideas and act as per your choice.

When your mind is free from all bad ideas, you can say that your mind is full of energy to do a particular task and you are better able to achieve the success you deserve. The ideas imposed on you by others make your mind dependent. Extract something good from those ideas and let your own thinking work to bring something positive out of it. Make a good healthy decision out of it. Hence, independence of the mind is another important feature to bring about a change in the self on your journey towards success and a peaceful life.

Independent are those who are truly independent of the mind and the body. They have exclusive ideas that can benefit the humanity at large. Also independent are those who choose the best for themselves and others. This life is yours, you are the driver. When you drive a vehicle, you have to follow certain rules, but your mind is free to take the little decisions relating to your driving skills while staying within the limitations, i.e., following the traffic rules. This is the best example for understanding the independence of your mind.

Let your mind fly and be free of the boundaries of negativity. You will feel light and uplifted. Meditation is a good method to make your mind more independent. I have seen people praying in holy shrines and chanting prayers for the whole day, but after sometime, they start scolding and cursing their children and their own life. This comes from the fear and slavery of the mind. Do not make your mind a slave to the others. You cannot please everyone in this world. What matters is that you please your own mind and fill it with values that will automatically bring back to you what is yours.

Choose the path of truth and sincerity; you will become more independent. Think good of yourself, and the people will think good of you too. Do not make yourself dependent on others. Create your own sources to support yourself. On your journey towards success, you might have to do petty jobs, but they are essential to support your life. You performance matters more than money. Bless whosoever comes into your life, or helps you a little, or even one who doesn't help at all. When you grow in virtue and value, all the money that you desire will be yours.

The journey towards success and change of the self is not that difficult. It is in the trick that when you think on it independently and work on it, you will get success.

Moreover, this is the universal truth. The vibrations that you give off in the universe definitely come back to you. Monitor each and every thought of yours and work on each and every act that you do. The more independent you are, the more successful you will be. Independence of the mind makes you self disciplined and more confident. Free your mind from all the bad ideas and negative thoughts.

Don't ever seek the intoxication of alcohol, drugs, smoking or any other such substances. Be intoxicated with the values of your mind. Find bliss in the love given to you by your family, your spouse, children, parents, friends, etc. Most importantly, you are independent to achieve any height you wish to attain in your life. Your soul and mind are free from all burdens and sins. Being financially independent is your right. Create opportunities for yourself to lead a successful and blissful life.

Exercise 18

Recall a few past events when you forgave someone who had wronged you in the past and mark it in list A. Then, make a list B where you write about your forgiveness. Write here the names of those persons who have been gentle to you and overlooked your mistakes. Example; your mother, father, friends etc.

List A

1.
2.
3.
4.
5.
6.
7.
8.

List B

1.
2.
3.
4.
5.
6.
7.
8.

Write about the incidents where you learnt to become more tolerant. List it below:

1.
2.
3.
4.
5.
6.
7.
8.

Make a list of the times when you felt independent and took your decisions independently.

1.
2.
3.
4.
5.
6.
7.
8.

Chapter 19

HEALTH IS THE ENTHUSIASM TO WORK

Health is both physical and mental. Health is the costliest thing in the world for a person who is suffering from an illness and the cheapest for the person who is healthy and well nourished. Fitness of the mind and the body are both very important for good health. A healthy mind lives in a healthy body.

You need a lot of energy to work throughout the day. From where do you get all that energy from? Have you ever thought of that? The answer is–right food, a natural pattern of sleeping and positive thoughts. Your health depends on you. Your thoughts and feelings play a vital role in keeping you fit too. Your thought pattern decides your health. A person who claims to be fit has a positive force in him which turns into positive energy. All diseases take birth first in your mind. It's how you damage your own health. Like all other life changing mantras, you can start from where you are. You are never too late to take care of your physical as well as mental health.

Beginning from where you are, you can take better care of your health. To maintain a better health, you can follow the advice of a doctor. You can learn exercises to maintain your health while also eating the right kind of food. There is an old saying, "An apple a day keeps the doctor away." Physical exercise in any form be it running, walking, swimming, dancing, cycling, etc, is very important. Thirty to forty minutes of walking at least five times a week is sufficient to maintain your health. Never force your body to do certain types of exercises all of a sudden. Always start slowly.

Exercise long and deep breathing. Inhale slowly, then exhale slowly. Repeat it at least ten times a day. Again, you can start doing this three to five times a day first. If it does not suit your body, then do not try it further and stop. Your physical and mental health should be your priority. If you are physically tired and stressed out despite being successful and wealthy, you will not feel any real happiness and you will be unable to enjoy your wealth too. Wealth without health is nothing. For enjoying your wealth, you need a good health.

Money cannot buy good health for you. When your health is in a critical situation, only your mind with its positive will power can bring your health back. With the strength of your mind, you can come out of even the worst health related situations. The medications also work better when you have a strong will power to get out of your poor health. Go ahead and start taking better care of your health from today itself. Take your health as a serious issue. Your body has its own repairing and healing system. Positive thoughts, good feelings, a company of positive people, the right medication and meditation can all bring you out of the worst diseases like cancer, tuberculosis, etc. Your will power provides you the energy to fight even the deadliest of diseases.

Give priority to your health. As long as your mind is polluted with negative thoughts, the attainment of good health will be out of your control. Negative thoughts produce bad energy that attracts all type of diseases as well as depression. Help yourself by believing in the notion that God helps those who help themselves. A sound mind lives in a healthy and fit body, free from all ailments.

Being lethargic is generally the main cause of one's bad health. Sometimes, when you wake up late in the morning, you feel lazy despite having slept for long hours. Your body and mind do not feel fresh either. You feel pain or stiffness around your neck, back or joints. Similarly, your mind feels tired too, as even during your extra hours of sleep, your mind did not stop working and its process of producing waste thoughts was at its peak. The excess of waste thoughts produced by your mind, i.e. bad thoughts or an unnecessary preoccupation with them do not let your brain rest. Thus, you feel lazy or drowsy the whole day. For that, you need to correct your sleeping pattern.

Nature has provided you with automatic functions inside your body, which you need to manage and maintain. There are majorly eleven systems inside a human body, which include circulatory, respiratory, digestive, excretory, nervous, endocrine, immune, skeleton, integumentary, muscular and reproductive systems. All functions of the body work simultaneously to keep the body in perfect condition. To make this happen, you should take proper food in the right proportion, work out a little and maintain good thoughts in your mind.

Reading good books makes your mind healthy. Company of good friends is also good for mental health. No matter what you are, where you are, health is always important. A person full of energy is a healthy person. Your body may have some imperfections or diseases from birth, but you invite many diseases through your sedentary lifestyle. You must have seen how even the people who are physically challenged improve their overall condition to participate and win the Paralympics. They are great example-setters for us all. Start from where you are it's never too late.

Jono Lancaster has Treacher Collins syndrome, a genetic disorder that affects the development of facial bones. He was abandoned by his parents only thirty six hours after his birth. A woman named Jean Lancaster adopted and raised him. His intelligence and development otherwise was as normal as any other boy his age. Since a very young age, Jono was constantly teased. He was desperate to have friends. He had no confidence. He often bought sweets for others kids so that they would like him. As he grew up, he started consuming alcohol. He was often lonely and depressed. When he was nineteen years old, he met a girl named Laura. This was the turning point of his life. Laura's love changed his attitude towards life. Jono gained more confidence in himself. His doctors suggested constructive surgeries to him, but he declined. Now, he has accepted and is happy with his appearance. He says, "God made me this way. I'm proud of who I am." With this positivism, Jono Lancaster is now actively involved in spreading awareness about Treacher Collins syndrome and Adult Autism all over the world. Today, he is an inspiration for many. He never lets his inner light be dimmed because of his appearance.

Eat light, keep fit and keep moving yourself throughout the day. Health is everything.

There is a popular saying that sleeping early and waking up early is good for your health. This is well analysed and justified by various sleep analysts. Your body has a biological clock that helps regulate your various body functions, including your sleeping time. A famous health advisor studied the pattern of sleeping and divided sleep into various sets to explain what the perfect time to sleep was for good health.

From 11.00 p.m. to 03.00 a.m., most of your blood is concentrated in your liver. Your liver gets larger when filled with more blood. This is the time when your body undergoes a detoxification process. If you do not sleep at this time, the detoxification process will not be carried out properly. If you sleep at 11.00 p.m., you'll have four hours to detoxify your body. If you sleep at 12.00 a.m., you'll have three hours only; if you sleep at 1.00 a.m., you'll have only two, and if you sleep at 2.00 a.m., you'll have just one hour for this process. If you regularly sleep at 3.00 a.m., your body will get no time to detoxify itself. The toxins will accumulate in your body over time and eventually attract many dreadful diseases. Going to sleep late and waking up late is very bad for your health.

From 3.00 a.m. to 5.00 a.m., most of the blood is concentrated in your lungs. It is the best time to exercise and breathe in fresh air, preferably in a garden. From 5.00 a.m. to 7.00 a.m., most of your blood is concentrated in your large intestine. Pass out all the unwanted poop from your large intestine at this time and prepare your body to absorb more nutrition throughout the day. From 7.00 a.m. to 9.00 a.m. most of your blood is concentrated in your stomach. Have your breakfast at this time, the most important meal of the day. Take all the nutrients that you require from your breakfast itself. Not having proper breakfast can cause a lot of health problems for you in future. People living in villages who work on farms are so healthy because they go to sleep early and wake-up early, following their natural biological clock.

Never curse your body. Always bless yourself and accept yourself as you are created by the Creator. You yourself need the maximum blessings, so bless yourself. You should also always keep in your mind that you are already blessed. Even if you do not have conventionally beautiful looks, you are the most beautiful and blessed one. No matter if you are tall, short, fair, dark, lean or fat, love yourself and take care of your health. Consider the people who are born handicapped but still have the spark to live with dignity. They make their presence in the society by doing something great.

Helen Keller was born deaf and blind but with the help of the greatest gift of Braille introduced by Louis Braille she turned to be a great author, political activist and lecturer. Do positive things for your health. You become whatever you feel. If you feel a complex with anything regarding your body, you need to change your perspective right away. Women of all shades of skin tone have won international competitions like Miss World and Miss Universe. No matter how your body is, take care of your overall health. What is most important is to love and bless yourself, only then can others do that for you.

"To be successful you do not need beautiful face and heroic body, what you need is skilful mind and ability to perform."–Rowan Atkinson

Perform with full confidence and focus, and success will be yours. In your success, your body, mind, thinking, feeling, living, health, vision, perspective, nature, knowledge, tolerance, patience, i.e., everything related to you participates. Your body needs your utmost care, as does your mind. If you take care of your mind properly, more than half the task relating to your body is already done. You will feel like a pure soul.

Everybody is different. All individuals have different qualities. There is no need of comparison at any stage. Make yourself feel as if you are the best human being. No doubt, all human beings are the best in their own way. You are not born to be sick or feeble. Make yourself strong through your will power, a proper diet and exercise. Start living from today itself the quality of life that you wish to have. Yesterday has already gone, it was not in your hands; tomorrow is yet to come and again it is not in your hands, but today is present-a lovely gift that is in your hands. Do not wait for tomorrow. Do whatever you want to do in this moment, start from today. Start taking better care of your health from today. Do not worry if you are diabetic, hypertensive, a cardiac patient, a cancer patient, have AIDS or any other severe disease. You can fight, rather 'beat' that disease with your will power, positive thinking, eating healthier, living better and medication.

You should also meditate for about ten to fifteen minutes once or twice a day. You have to convey to yourself that you have a perfect and healthy body. Do not think about diseases again and again. While taking your medicine, think and bless yourself that this medicine is perfect, life giving and full of healing properties. Be thankful that your disease has been diagnosed well in time. You have every power within yourself to heal yourself. Focus on your health and well being.

Lord Buddha has said, "To keep the body in good health is a duty otherwise we shall not be able to keep our mind strong and clear."

At many medico-centers, I have found it written, 'Take care of your body, it is the only place you live in.' Only a healthy mind can think of a healthy successful life. Joyce Meyer said, " I believe that the greatest gift you can give your family and the world is a healthy you." So don't let down the famous saying, "Health is wealth."

Exercise 19

Make a list of your good and bad eating habits. Write your bad habits on small paper slips then tear those off one by one.

Make a list of the good things that you should eat to lead a healthier life.

1.

2.

3.

4.

5.

6.

7.

8.

Chapter 20

YOUR PLANNING AND HIS PLANNING

Planning is an important action required to put any of your ideas or dreams into reality. Planning is an important function required to accomplish your goal. Plan whatever you want to be in life. For that, you have to think clearly. A vague idea creates confusion in your mind. One should be clear in one's mind regarding what one wants to be. There should be no confusion. Many a times, you have so many ideas in your mind that confuse you. In such a case, you must work on one idea at a time. Dream about that again and again with your eyes open; visualize your dream.

Add the same to the pattern of your life. Live the dream as if it's real and you will one day see it coming true. Plan it today itself before another idea distracts you tomorrow, or the day after tomorrow. This process is continuous and you shall never be able to plan what to do unless you start right away. Just do it now, put it into action. Time is short to make your idea into reality. Focus on your idea, dream it, plan it, implement it-nothing is impossible.

Few days ago, I got a chance to visit Malaysia and Singapore. The buildings I saw there, particularly in Kuala-Lumpur and Singapore, really impressed and fascinated me. During your childhood, you must have gotten a chance to play with blocks or empty matchboxes, balancing them one on top of the other to make buildings as imagined by you. Such were the thoughts that came to my mind when I saw the buildings there. It makes me wonder how an architect even imagined the plan and the other executed the idea to put to reality.

No matter what you dream, it can become a reality if you work hard enough on it. Planning is the most important aspect of moving ahead on the journey of transformation. You must plan, regardless of whether things go according to your plan or not. If things go the other way, accept them as the will of the Almighty, the Universe, and have faith that the Supreme is planning something better and special for you. Believing, loving, accepting and having faith in Him makes you work with more zeal and zest. If you plan your dream with positivity and start taking all those steps which are necessary for the achievement of your dream, He–the Almighty, will put in His powerful force too to make your dreams come true.

Walk a step forward with faith in yourself and Him, and you will find that He is there with you in every step you take. Plan for your positive dreams with a positive mind, since your sub-conscious mind accepts whatever your conscious mind does. If you make negative plans, your sub-conscious mind will start believing it as true and will start working on it. It's in your hands whether you make your destiny or mar it.

Do not wait for opportunities to knock at your door, create your own opportunities. Every step that you take is an opportunity; take it with full confidence.

When you go for a trip, you always plan your itinerary in advance, from boarding the bus or car or train or plane at the beginning, all the way till the end of your journey. During this journey, you keep safe your tickets, passport, transfer documents, etc., of the places where you are intended to go. Why not then should you take care of your body and mind that play a pivotal role in your life's journey. Think back on the time when you started this journey of life. As a young child, your parents helped you, then your siblings, your elders, friends, relatives, colleagues, etc. all came in to execute their roles in making your life's journey easier.

When you visit far off places for a holiday, you feel relaxed and enjoy the place, as well as the various things that it has to offer, and keep those in your memories. Why don't you enjoy your life in the same way? Plan it from today itself. Decide today what you want to be in life. Many ideas will confuse you. Comparing yourself with others will confuse you even more, but jealousy at others will never lead you to live a proper and blissful life. Such vices occupy the lowest rung of human attributes and contribute in no way to the transformation of soul. Love yourself, talk to yourself gently recognize your qualities, as nobody else knows you better than yourself. You have the ability and capability to do many things. Recognize your tastes and likings then start working on them one by one. Plan your dreams in the right direction. Start living as if you have already fulfilled your dreams. You are a very special, intelligent, knowledgeable, loveable, blissful, peaceful and powerful creature of His creation. Believe in yourself and plan the right things for yourself.

No matters how old you may be, you can still achieve anything. In this book of mine, I have given so many examples of persons who started late in their lives and reached the top, proving themselves to be very successful. There is no fixed law that states that a person can only become successful in life if he starts early. If a person start very early in life, the chances of him/her facing failure are more. Age is no bar for your dreams and planning is very important for all your dreams.

Every plan needs action, though. There is no need to suppress your weaknesses or feelings, rather make them your strengths. Life is a journey. Fears have no place in it, so be positive. Plan your schedule today itself. Try to follow and implement it in your life. If you fail on the first day, do not worry. Even if you fail on the second, third, fourth, fifth, sixth.... or whatever day, further, don't worry then either.

Make a new plan that suits you more then try to implement it. If it works on the first, second, third day and so on, praise yourself for having done well. Tell yourself that you can achieve anything. Try to think about your goals more often and spend time with the people whom you like the most. Do not think of those people who are not in your good books. Don't try to hurt the persons who have been wrong to you, as it will deplete your energy. Think of a good quality they have and the good times that you've spent with them, and forget the rest. Make your mind free of all burdens only then can you complete the journey of transformation of your soul.

Choose the best for yourself. Plan for that and He will help you. Create a new vision. Your subconscious mind is very strong and intelligent, but it believes things to be true as you present them to it. Make a list of ideas and write them down in a journal. Note the ideas that proved to be true and the goals, however small, that you have managed to achieve till date. Be grateful for them and do not stop; keep going. Set small goals initially; plan for them then act to achieve them.

Say, you are reading a book that has two hundred pages. You can set a particular time to finish reading it, be it a week or ten days. Divide the pages by days of the week. This will make it easier for you to finish reading the book within the time limit set by you. It is the same if you want to learn swimming, some particular dance, a song, or any other thing. Normally, your coach may fix a period of two months for that. You set a time limit for yourself that is a week less than two months. This will inspire you to work with more enthusiasm and will enable you to learn the thing before the time set by others.

If you need to learn driving perfectly, the driving tutor may give you a month's time to learn. Make sure that you do it in twenty one days. This way, you will enjoy learning for the remaining days, which will be sufficient for your practice. Make plans first, only then will it be possible for you to achieve a goal. Planning is as important as setting the goal and then taking action upon it. If you want to go to some other country, you first need to have a plan for it and then move in that direction. Dream, imagine a plan, put it into action, focus on it, believing that you have already achieved it, and it shall take you towards success.

Every child, no matter where he is born and to whom he is born, has to learn certain skills. Even those who beg on the road have learned the skill to do so. During small talk with people we know, we often hear or ask the question, "What are you doing nowadays?" People often respond to it by saying 'nothing'. This 'nothing' really surprises me, as to how could a person be so free.

Before I started writing this book, I had done multiple assignments at different stages. Today, when somebody asks me, "Are you at home? Not doing a job?" it amuses me and makes me wonder, "Are people, especially women, who stay at home truly free?"I find myself busy the whole day, doing all kinds of creative things. For the last three years, I have been a full-time home maker. Is it no small job. The daily tasks involve deciding the menu for the day, giving instructions to the staff at home, taking care of everything relating to the house, the cleaning, washing, dusting, etc., handling all the market related chores and so on.

Home makers are big planners. They have to plan each and everything in advance, not only for themselves, but for the entire family, guests, relatives and friends. One can't ever controvert with one's own planning. Plan in the direction in which you want to work. If you want to build yourself a wooden table, you will need to collect a hammer, nails, wood, etc. Initially, you will have to draw a plan on paper, record the measurements–its height, width, length, and consider the size of nails to be used. If you plan for a table, but bring entirely different articles in the preparation, such as soap, paper, colour, etc., how will you be able to put your plan into action?

Exercise 20

Write about your planning towards your goal in a journal. List the steps you need to take to accomplish your goal.

1.

2.

3.

4.

5.

Final stage: When you finish all the initial steps. You will accomplish your goal. Achieve whatever you want to achieve with positive effort in the right direction.

Bonus Chapter

EXPECTATIONS

By Suha Soni

Since the moment you come into existence, a constant connection develops between you and other human beings. Now, let me take you back, way back to the day your parents got to know that you were about to become a part of this world soon. Your parents started expecting from that very moment. Does that sound negative to you?

Let us now go a little ahead from that day, when the expectations began regarding whether it would be a girl or a boy, premature or on time, arrive via a normal birth or through a C-section, and so on. The baby has arrived, congratulations! Imagine yourself sleeping calmly in some cot in the neonatal ward, or right next to your mom. You were completely unaware of the world around you, but you could not stop yourself from being amazed by the new environment and the people. You also could not stop yourself from crying, or feeling hungry or pooping.

Despite all of this newness, you adjusted. You were expected to! You went home, fell sick, recovered from that sickness, grew older into a smart little infant who was both naughty and experimental. As you grew, what else grew? Yes, expectations. By the age of three, you were expected to join a school. You were still a kid with barely any idea of all that you were going through. All you knew is that whatever your parents did was the best. You loved them the most.

On the very first day of school, when either of your parents left you at the classroom door, you were filled with tears in your eyes. Suddenly just then, you met a stranger, your class teacher. She calmed you down and made you sit. You had the very first class of the little life that you had lived, and it was all so very new.

Why did I take you back there? Because that day, a cycle of endless expectations began. You were expected to be impeccably dressed, you were expected to poop and pee with prior notice, expected to finish your homework, expected to learn foreign languages, numbers and colours, expected to be respectful, make new friends, expected to be good and what not. As you were young, these expectations were small, but as you grew up, the expectations also grew.

Let's talk real now. Did these expectations really grow, or did your pessimism outgrow your positivity?

Think.

Let me put it simply for you. When you were a little kid, running around here and there, people had expectations from you back then as well. Now you would think those expectations as meaningless and trivial. My question then is: How old were you? If the expectations were small, so were you. At that time, they too were new to you. The scenario today is that those expectations have grown with you and with time, but you're an adult now too. There is a linearly increasing graph between your age and the expectations from you.

The next question: If it is a linear relationship between age and expectations, why are they turning me insane today, when they did not do so back then?

Your attitude

You have stopped smiling. You have stopped being open to new things and challenges. The society gives you different phases in life to build new relationships, when you are expected to fall in love and have a family of your own. By this time, you have already tackled the expectations of performing well in exams, going to college and getting a job. Stop here and ponder, you have started hating expectations now because you are no more a kid, and are afraid of making mistakes and being laughed at.

By all this, I want you to realize that expectations are not negative. They are a part of basic human existence and are as old as the history of mankind. The next time you walk by a street, look at the little children running around and enjoying themselves. This is what is required of an adult in today's era. Smile and be happy to accept all expectations. Do not be afraid of making mistakes. Mistakes are a part of life and can be tackled easily. Do not shirk from the idea of expectations. Expectations make humans more enthusiastic and focused. This is the very idea behind expectations.

Today, there are numerous cases of suicide, depression and increasing divorces in our society. The culprit is usually expectations. Expectations are not negative, however, it is only our attitude towards them.

Every human being functions differently and it is difficult to expect that people will stop expecting. All you can do is that each time you feel that your life is becoming a sad cocktail of expectations, go back to your childhood and smile. Make yourself comfortable, confident and ready to commit mistakes. Do not blame the expectations, deal with them. They are only meant for you to become better than what you are right now. Also, never stop loving yourself or the people around you. Fall in love with their expectations, and handle them with love and care.

You are precious. Far more precious than any exam or any mistake.

Epilogue

The journey encapsulated in this book is actually my own. I never understood how all these things affected me before. As all other persons, I knew only two emotions–happy in good moments and sad in bad situations. But as I read some books and gained experiences through life, I understood the 'secret'. From that time onwards, I came to know why a person is sad all the time, or why he keeps waiting for moments of happiness to come into his life. Slowly, I learnt that all the happiness, sadness, nervousness and impulsiveness are always within us. We cannot put the blame on others for our sadness, failure, etc.

Repeated thinking of negative thoughts invite more of the same thoughts and allows them to settle down in our body and mind. Normally, we don't even invite those guests who disturb us or give us trouble, then why do we invite the negative feelings that trouble our mind, and let them make our mind and body sick. It's the truth. As long as we have a soul inside our body, we have life in it. So, it's our moral duty to keep our mind and body clean. People bathe daily and change into new and fresh clothes. What about the freshness of our mind? We brush our teeth daily, change clothes, wash our face, but the most important thing, our body, remains unclean despite all these rituals. Why?

Have you been to a religious place? The devotees clean and wash the place thoroughly, the stairs, the front and back yard, and the inner chamber with water and at some places, with milk too. What use is all that if we never clean our minds before going to such places of worship? The same is with our body. We shower from head to toe, but care less for our mind that thinks, gives directions, and decides everything for us. It remains constantly negative from morning till evening. The purity of mind is as important as washing or bathing our body.

Like our body excretes all wastage from itself, the mind needs to follow suit. Each and every chapter in this book is followed by a simple exercise that can help you do the same.

I hope that all I have learnt through the years of my life may benefit you. I am thankful to all those who were a part of my journey of writing this book. This book has been my childhood 'dream'. I never let the spark of writing fade away through all these years. I kept the light burning inside me. No doubt, it took me many years to reach my goal, but I finally wrote this book.

Finally, brethren,

whatsoever things are true, whatsoever things are honest, whatsoever things are just, whatsoever things are pure, whatsoever things are lovely, whatsoever things are of good report;

if they are virtue, and if there be any praise, think on these things.

- PHIL4:8
(The Bible)

About the Author

Ms. Roohi Soni was born and brought up in Chandigarh. Her schooling happened from different places as her father had a transferable job. She is an advocate by profession. She graduated from M. C. M. DAV College, Chandigarh and then went on to get a post-graduation degree in English literature from Govt. College, Hoshiarpur. Both these colleges come under Punjab University, Chandigarh. She did her graduation in Law from Guru Nanak Dev University, Amritsar.

She got married to Sanjeev Soni, advocate, Punjab and Haryana High court, at a place near Amritsar. She is now a mother of two. Her daughter is currently pursuing M.B.B.S, while her son is doing B.Com LLB. The place where she got married had very few English medium schools in those days, so she opened one for the children in that area.

Since she was an advocate, she got appointed as the court auctioneer by the Punjab and Haryana High Court. Thereafter, she became the President [JUDGE] District Consumer Disputes Redressal Forum. Presently, she is practicing as an advocate at Punjab and Haryana High Court.

In Praise of the Author...

An ethereal soul, Roohi Soni is a true feminist and a loving mother. She has held various posts as an advocate and President(judge) and had been a beacon of truth and honesty. Like a true Cancerian, she is kind, wise and a liberal soul whom we all can learn a great deal from. Roohi Soni has vast experience in the matters of the world and the heart, and is not just a helpful person but a diligent observer of life too. I wish her all the best and I await her book.

Shabari Prasad Singh

Author - Borderline

Printed by Libri Plureos GmbH in Hamburg,
Germany